DIVE GUI

MALAYSIA

INCLUDING SABAH, SARAWAK AND SINGAPORE

JACK JACKSON

Series Consultant: Nick Hanna

**NEW
HOLLAND**

This third edition published in 2002 by
New Holland Publishers (UK) Ltd
London • Cape Town • Sydney • Auckland

86–88 Edgware Road	80 McKenzie Street	14 Aquatic Drive	218 Lake Road
London W2 2EA	Cape Town 8001	Frenchs Forest, NSW 2086	Northcote, Auckland
UK	South Africa	Australia	New Zealand

www.newhollandpublishers.com

10 9 8 7 6 5 4 3

ISBN 1 84330 238 1

Publishing manager: Jo Hemmings
Series editor: Kate Michell
Design concept: Philip Mann, ACE Ltd
Design/cartography: ML Design, London
Index: Alex Corrin
Production: Joan Woodroffe

Reproduction by Unifoto, Cape Town
Printed and bound in Singapore by Tien Wah Press (Pte) Ltd

All photographs by Jack Jackson with the exception of the following:
Gerald Cubitt 10, 36, 46, 71, 86, 88, 107, 118; Footprints 43, 117 (Nick Hanna), 162 top right
(Paul Naylor), 13, 94, 101 (Philip Waldock); Jill Gocher 15; R. Mod Noh 8, 15; Linda Pitkin title
page, 25, 81; Planet Earth 162 bottom left (Peter Scoones); Travel Ink 150 (Ronald Badkin).

Front cover: *Diver and mixed corals.*
Spine: *Clownfish (Amphiprion Rubrocintus).*
Back cover top: *Dive boat at Pulau Redang, Terangganu.*
Back cover bottom: *Author Jack Jackson on live-aboard dive boat.*
Title page: *Exploring a shallow reef.*
Contents page: *Divers against a foreground of soft corals.*

AUTHOR'S ACKNOWLEDGEMENTS

Writing a guide book of this nature requires the help and goodwill of local experts, dive operators and divemasters who contribute their time and knowledge. Of the many people who helped me with my diving and research in Malaysia and Singapore, I would like to give special thanks and appreciation to:

- Clement Lee, Randy Davis and Ron Holland, Directors of Borneo Divers, who organized my diving at Labuan and Sangalaki
- Neil Antrum and Jon Rees for their guiding on these dives
- Veronica Lee and Danny Chin, of Pulau Sipadan Resort, who patiently endured the requests of a photographer who considers his photography before anything else!
- Andrew Chong, for showing me the diving in Tunku Abdul Rahman Marine Park and Pulau Tiga Park and for sharing his wealth of knowledge on Layang-Layang
- Daniel D'Orville, for masterminding my diving in Peninsular Malaysia and introducing me to other kindred spirits there
- Lawrence Lee, who, with the help of T.H. Foo of Redang Pelangi Resort, handled the logistics and collected together diving equipment, transport, a boat, fuel and crew so that he could show me the diving around Pulau Redang
- Ramli Chik and Stephen Ng of Perhentian Island Resort, for helping me discover the diving around Pulau Perhentian
- William and Ruby Ong, Directors of Pro Diving Services, Singapore, for their infectious enthusiasm for diving and conservation in Singaporean waters
- Michael Lim, Director of Sharkeys Dive & Adventure, for further information on Singapore diving
- Chan Chee Sing and Azman Sulaiman, for helping me with the diving around Pulau Tioman
- Raja Iskandar, Assistant Director of the Malaysian Tourism Promotion Board in London, for his help with the project; Malaysian Airlines, for flying me out to and around Malaysia
- Susan Abraham, Sarala Aikanathan and Junaidi Payne, of WWF Malaysia, for answering my many awkward questions
- Captain Sim Yong Wah, for his knowledge of some areas that are rarely dived
- And, last but not least, Michael Wong, Paul Street and Paul Etgart, for goading me into making my first visit to Malaysia's underwater paradise

PUBLISHERS' ACKNOWLEDGEMENTS

The publishers gratefully acknowledge the generous assistance during the compilation of this book of the following:

Nick Hanna for his involvement in developing the series and consulting throughout and Dr Elizabeth M. Wood for acting as Marine Consultant and contributing to The Marine Environment.

PHOTOGRAPHY

The author's photographs were taken using Nikonos III, Nikonos V, Nikon F-801s and Nikon F-90 cameras. The Nikonos cameras were used with 15mm and 28mm Underwater Nikkor lenses. The Nikon F-801s and Nikon f-90/90x cameras were housed in either of three waterproof aluminium housings and used with 14mm, 24mm, 55mm macro and 105mm macro lenses. Two of these housings were manufactured by the Austrian company Subal and the other by the Swiss company Hugyfot.

   All the photographs were taken with the addition of electronic flash to replace the colour filtered out by the water. An Oceanic 2001 Strobe was used with the Nikonos III and either a Nikon SB-24 Speedlight in a Subal housing or a Hugyfot/Subtronic Hugystrobe HST300 Professional was used with the other cameras. The film stock used was, variously, Fujichrome Velvia, Fujichrome RDP and Kodak Ektachrome Elite/Panther.

INTRODUCTION TO MALAYSIA AND SINGAPORE

Malaysia

Malaysia has everything: friendly people, long empty beaches, coral reefs, beautiful scenery, islands, mountains and hill resorts, and nowadays hundreds of golf courses. The weather is marvellous too; with very few exceptions, temperatures are always about 28°C (82°F). The nation is a confederation of thirteen states plus two federal territories: Wilayah (around Kuala Lumpur) and Pulau Labuan. Nine of the eleven Peninsular states have sultans, and every five years the sultans elect one of their number to reign as King of Malaysia. The states of Sabah and Sarawak in East Malaysia (North Borneo) were not part of the nation when Malaya (as it then was) became independent in 1957, joining the new-formed Federation of Malaysia in 1963 along with Singapore. Singapore left the federation in 1965; Sabah and Sarawak remain within it but retain a greater degree of local administration than the eleven Peninsular states.

In 1981 the government of Prime Minister Dato' Seri Mahathir bin Mohammad came to power, ushering in an era of stability, industrialization and economic growth. Dr Mahathir's policies have attracted foreign investors, and Malaysia is now one of the most stable, prosperous and progressive countries in Southeast Asia. Richly endowed with natural resources, it has the world's largest tin deposits, extensive oil and gas reserves and rainforests full of valuable tropical hardwoods. Until fairly recently the economy was heavily dependent on these resources and on plantation crops: rubber, pepper, cocoa and oil palm. However, dwindling world prices hit the value of plantation crops hard. The best prices are now command-ed by oil palm, although the AIDS pandemic in other countries has caused an increase in demand for natural rubber, the main constituent of surgical rubber gloves and condoms.

All modern communications are available: even the remotest island resort has a mobile telephone, and elsewhere virtually every businessman carries a mobile or hand telephone at all times. The rapidly growing tourist industry is now, after manufacturing and oil, the economy's third-largest earner of foreign income.

Opposite: *The modern high-rise city of Kuala Lumpur by night.*
Above: *View across the bay to Singapore from Sentosa Island.*

The logging industry has earned the country notoriety among environmentalists, but much of Malaysia's land area is still forested – although not necessarily with primary rainforest – and the government has been enthusiastically promoting ecotourism. There are several beautiful National Parks, and in Sarawak the cultures of several forest tribes have remained remarkably intact.

THE LAND

Malaysia consists of two distinct regions separated by a 500km (310-mile) stretch of the South China Sea. Peninsular or West Malaysia is a finger of land below Thailand, extending 800km (500 miles) from north to south, with Singapore at its southern tip. East Malaysia is most of the northern part of the island of Borneo.

The island of Pulau Tioman, off the east coast of Peninsular Malaysia, is a tropical paradise of golden sand and blue sea.

Most of Peninsular Malaysia is covered in tropical rainforest, especially its northern half, where there are also high mountains. The western side of the peninsula has long fertile plains descending to the sea. The mountains descend more steeply on the eastern side, and there are many more beaches there. The central area is sparsely populated.

East Malaysia is divided into Sabah and Sarawak, the latter surrounding the two small enclaves that are the Sultanate of Brunei. Both states are covered in dense tropical rainforest and, particularly Sarawak, have large river systems. Mount Kinabalu (4094m; 13,432ft), in Sabah, is the highest mountain in that part of Southeast Asia lying between the Himalayas and New Guinea.

Geologically, both the peninsula and Borneo are part of the Sunda shelf, although the mountains of the peninsula are older than those of Borneo. The granite pluton that is Mount Kinabalu began pushing up through the sedimentary rocks of the Crocker Range about two million years ago.

FLORA AND FAUNA

The core areas of tropical rainforest in Peninsular Malaysia, Borneo and New Guinea are possibly the most diverse of the world's terrestrial ecosystems; by way of example, in a mere 1ha (2½ acres) of Malaysian rainforest there may be as many as 176 species of tree of bole-diameter over 10cm (4in). This rainforest, dating back some 130 million years, has been cited as the oldest in the world, but this statement has to be qualified: it and its vegetation must have undergone radical change many times during its history in accordance with prevailing geological processes, climate and sea-levels. Peninsular Malaysia has more than 8000 species of flowering plants while the island of Borneo has more than 11,000, most of which – including the world's largest flower, *Rafflesia* – occur in Sabah and Sarawak.

There are some 200 species of mammals, including the Asiatic Elephant, Sumatran Rhinoceros, leopards and clouded leopards. Peninsular Malaysia has a few tigers left and

TRAVELLING TO AND IN MALAYSIA AND SINGAPORE

Getting to Malaysia and Singapore and travelling around once there is generally straight-forward unless you are heading for a very remote destination. Transport and communications are efficient and travel information is readily available. This section provides a summary of useful travel details to help you plan your trip; for more specific information check the Regional Directory at the end of each regional section in the book or contact your nearest tourist office.

HEALTH

A certificate of vaccination against yellow fever is necessary for visitors coming from endemic zones. Immunizations against hepatitis-A, tetanus, typhoid and polio are recommended. Malaysia and Singapore are clean countries: the tap water in towns and resorts is safe to drink, and freshly cooked food and peeled fruit are safe to eat. Food cooked in front of you at roadside stalls and small restaurants can be safer to eat than that in luxury hotels, where it is often cooked earlier and then reheated. The risk of AIDS is present, although less so than in some neighbouring countries. Malaria is prevalent in Southeast Asia, so do not neglect to take sensible precautions.

Medical insurance

Malaysia and Singapore have modern medical facilities, but you cannot expect to find them in remote areas. It is always wise to buy a travel and medical insurance policy that includes repatriation by Air Ambulance in case of a serious accident or illness. If you do not have a specialist diving insurance policy, make sure that you pay the extra premium on your travel and medical insurance to cover diving activities.

Recompression (Hyperbaric) Chambers

For information on recompression chambers in Malaysia and Singapore see *Diving and Snorkelling in Malaysia and Singapore* (page 33).

Opposite: *Kuala Lumpur's Moorish railway station, built by the British in 1910.*
Above: *View from the high-speed ferry on its way to Batam Island off Singapore.*

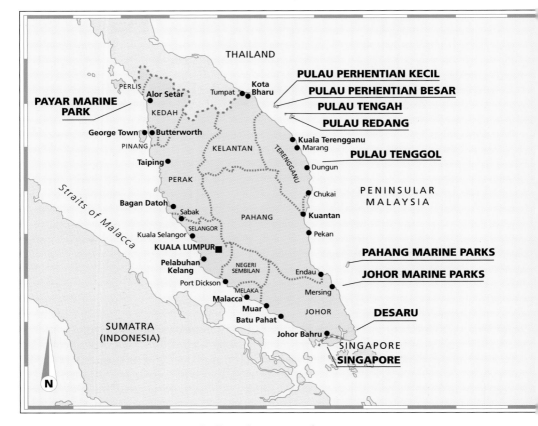

Malaysia

ARRIVING

By air: Peninsular Malaysia's main gateway, served by 27 international airlines, is the new Kuala Lumpur International Airport (KLIA), which was opened in 1998 at Sepang, 50km (31 miles) south of Kuala Lumpur. Scheduled flights are also available to Langkawi, Pulau Pinang and Kota Kinabalu. **By rail:** Trains from Bangkok run down the main Malaysian west-coast line via Butterworth (for Pulau Pinang) to Kuala Lumpur. **By road:** Long-distance express buses link major towns and cities in Malaysia with Singapore and destinations in Thailand. **By sea:** High-speed catamarans operate scheduled services linking Pulau Pinang and Langkawi on Malaysia's west coast with Medan in Sumatra and Phuket in Thailand.

ENTRY FORMALITIES

Your passport should be valid for at least six months from your date of entry into Malaysia. Visas are not required for UK protected persons, Commonwealth citizens (except Indians) or citizens of the Republic of Ireland, Liechtenstein, the Netherlands, San Marino and Switzerland. Citizens of Belgium, Denmark, Finland, France, Germany, Iceland, Italy, Luxembourg, Norway, Sweden and the USA may stay up to three months without a visa, so long as they are not working. Citizens of ASEAN countries do not require visas for visits not exceeding one month. Citizens of most other countries may visit for up to 14 days without a visa, except for those of Cambodia, Eastern Europe, the Commonwealth of Independent

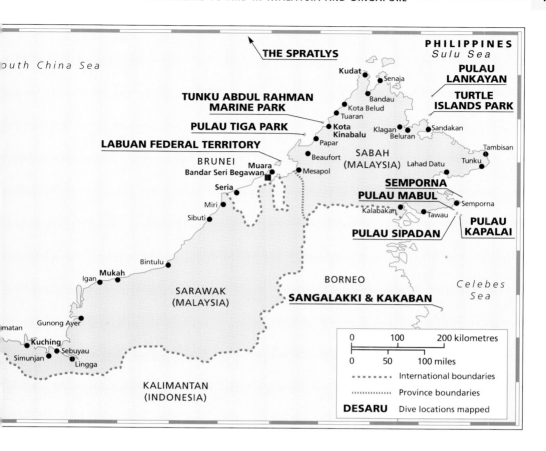

States, Laos and Vietnam, who must obtain visas in advance of their arrival from their nearest Malaysian Diplomatic Mission or from the British Consular Representative in countries where there are no Malaysian representatives. On arrival visitors receive a one-month visitor's permit; Commonwealth citizens can get a two-month permit if required. You must keep this with you until you leave. Visitors' permits issued on entry to Peninsular Malaysia are not automatically valid for entry into Sabah and Sarawak. Visitors have to go through immigration again, even though the flight is an internal one. There is a similar check on exit from Labuan. To visit any national park, or to take an up-river trip in Sarawak, you require a permit from the national or state parks office.

Customs
The duty-free allowances are 200 cigarettes, 50 cigars or 250 grams of tobacco, perfume not exceeding 200 ringgits in value, and 1 litre of liquor or wine. There is no limit on

LOCAL TRAVEL AGENTS IN KUALA LUMPUR

All hotels will act as agents for city tours. For tours around Malaysia:

Diethelm Travel Malaysia Box # 18, Wisma Selangor Dredging, 5th Floor, West Block 142-C Jalan Ampang, 50450 Kuala Lumpur; tel 03-4667878/fax 03-2616058; e-mail inb@dtm.po.my web site http://www.diethelm-travel.com

Iten Tours & Travel Sdn Bhd 3rd Floor, 7 Jalan Barat, 46200 Petaling Jaya, Selangor; tel 03-7569507/fax 03-7563613

Reliance Travel Agencies 3rd Floor, Sungei Wang Plaza; tel 03-2486022

still cameras, but visitors bringing in video equipment may have to pay a refundable deposit for temporary importation. You are not allowed to bring in weapons or pornography. The trafficking of illegal drugs carries the death penalty. Export permits are required for arms, ammunition, explosives, animals and plants, platinum, precious stones and jewellery (except for reasonable personal effects), antiques, poisons, drugs and vehicles.

All travellers are now required to fill in a Travellers Declaration Form (TDF) on arrival and present it again to the Immigration Officer on departure. Residents and non-residents are allowed to bring in not more than 1,000 ringgits in cash and an unlimited amount of foreign currency. Non-residents are only allowed to take out amounts less than or equivalent to the sums they have declared upon entry.

Airline concession
Malaysian Airlines used to offer an airline concession, available on request, of 30kg (66 pounds) extra baggage allowance for divers. This was cancelled in 1993.

MONEY
The Malaysian unit of currency is the ringgit (= 100 sen), although local people always refer to it as the `dollar' and write it as $ (or M$). Most credit cards are widely accepted; credit-card fraud occurs as in any other country. Travellers' cheques are likewise widely accepted, as are cash notes of the world's major trading currencies — especially the US dollar. Banks with currency-exchange facilities can be hard to find and transactions there are generally very slow; legal money changers are usually easier and quicker to use and offer the same rates of exchange as the banks for travellers' cheques — often better rates for large-denomination cash notes. A government directive states that only foreign unmarked cash notes in perfect condition are acceptable, so if you are planning to take currency of your country of domicile ask your bank for clean, unmarked notes. All travellers are now required to fill in a Travellers Declaration Form (TDF) on arrival and present it again to the Immigration Officer on departure. Non-residents are allowed to bring in not more than 1,000 ringgits in cash and an unlimited amount of foreigh currency. Non-residents are only allowed to take out amounts les than or equivalent to the sums they have declared upon entry. These forms are available at all entry and exit points, including airports, or may be obtained in advance from Malaysian Embassies and High Commissions.

ACCOMMODATION
A wide range of accommodation to suit all tastes and budgets is on offer in Malaysia, though facilities are limited at some of the remoter dive locations. Suggestions for where to stay are given in the Regional Directory at the end of each regional section. If you need to stay in Kuala Lumpur, refer to the fact panel above.

HOTELS IN KUALA LUMPUR

Try to find accommodation within walking distance of the centre to avoid rush hour traffic jams. There are countless hotels; here are just a few:

Upper Price Range
Kuala Lumpur Hilton Jalan Sultan Ismail, PO Box 10577, 50718 Kuala Lumpur; tel 03-2482322/fax 03-2442157; e-mail klhilton@tm.net.my; www.hilton.com/hotels

Shangri-La 11 Jalan Sultan Ismail, 50250 Kuala Lumpur; tel 03–2322388/fax 03-2301514; e-mail slkl@shangri-la.com; www.shangri-la.com:80/ shangri-la/hotels/20/20home.html

Medium Price Range
Hotel Orkid 300 Jalan Pudu, 55100 Kuala Lumpur; tel 03-2448033/fax 03–2485177

Agora Hotel 106–110 Jalan Bukit Bintang, 55100 Kuala Lumpur; tel 03–2428133/fax 03–2427815

Lower Price Range
Cheng Traveller Lodge Jalan Utara, off Jalan Imbi; tel 03–9823960. Dormitory-style accommodation.

Kuala Lumpur International Youth Hostel 21 Jalan Kampung Attap, 50460 Kuala Lumpur; tel 03-2736870/fax 03-2741115

ELECTRICITY

The electricity supply is 220-240 volts/50 cycles, as used in Europe. Most electrical sockets are of the three-square-pin type used in the UK. Many hotels now have a system whereby the electricity can be switched on only if you have inserted a plastic token, permanently attached to the room key, into a slot in your room. This is obviously a nuisance if you wish to charge batteries or keep the air conditioning going while you are out! However, many of these systems can be kept switched on by putting a piece of stiff cardboard or plastic into the slot.

GETTING AROUND

Peninsular Malaysia has a good road system, a railway that runs its length from Thailand to Singapore and a good internal air-transport system. All are easy to use and relatively cheap. Some areas have rickshaws, but taxis are inexpensive, and better if you have a lot of luggage; if you take a taxi between towns you will be expected to pay as if it had a full complement of four passengers. There are good, cheap long-distance bus services, though those marked 'express' in fact stop for a meal every two hours and wait an hour or more at major bus stations. I have found long-distance bus drivers and taxi drivers remarkably helpful; bus drivers often drop me at a taxi rank near where I want to go, rather than taking me to the central bus station and taxi drivers often help me organize the next part of my journey. **Kuala Lumpur's** traffic comes to a standstill during the rush hours, so try to avoid those periods. There are regular ferry services to **Pulau Tioman** and **Pulau Perhentian** from the Peninsular mainland. If you do not have much luggage, air

FILM PROCESSING IN KUALA LUMPUR

KL has numerous mini-labs that process print film but E6-transparency processing is limited. Most listed below also handle E6 processing for photo-shops in the provinces.

Bakway Translide Sdn Bhd 1A Jalan 19/1, 46300 Petaling Jaya Selangor; tel 03-7574140/fax 03-7572712

Kemajuan Professional Lab (M) Sdn Bhd 14 Jalan 19/3, 46300 Petaling Jaya Selangor; tel 03–7554979/fax 03–7554106

Advert Studio 22/23B Lrz Rahim Kajai, 13 Taman Tun Dr Ismail, 60000 Kuala Lumpur; tel 03–7186133/fax 03–7182321

PP Foto Sdn Bhd Lot 122, First Floor, City Point, Dayabumi Complex, Jalan Sultan Hissammuddin, 50050 Kuala Lumpur; tel 03-2916626

MALAYSIA TOURIST OFFICES

The Malaysia Tourism Promotion Board (MTPB) has various offices all over Malaysia and in many different countries of the world. For further details contact the Head Office (address below).

Head Office
17th Floor Menara Dato' Onn, Putra World Trade Center, 45 Jalan Tun Ismail, 50480 Kuala Lumpur; tel 03-2935188/fax 03-2935884; e-mail tourism@tourism.gov.my; www.tourism.gov.my

Sabah
Ground Floor EON CMG Life Building, No. I Jalan Sagunting, 88000 Kota Kinabalu; tel 088-248698/fax 088-241764; e-mail mtpbbki@tourism.gov.my

Sarawak
2nd Floor Rugayah Building, Jalan Song Thian Cheok, 93100 Kuching; tel 082-246575/fax 082-246442; e-mail mtpbkch@tourism.gov.my

Overseas Offices
Australia
Tourist Development Corporation Malaysia, 65 York Street, Sydney, NSW 2000, Australia; tel 672-2994441/fax 672-92622026; e-mail amir@access.com.au

Germany
Tourist Development Corporation Malaysia, Rossmarkt 11, 60311 Frankfurt Am Main, Germany; tel 069-283782/fax 069-285215; e-mail mtpb.frankfurt@arcormail.de

Singapore
Tourist Development Corporation Malaysia, 10 Collyer Quay, #01-06 & 18-02 Ocean Building, Singapore 049315; tel 02-5326321/fax 02-5356650; e-mail mtpb.singapore@tourism.gov.my

UK
Tourist Development Corporation Malaysia, 57 Trafalgar Square, London WC2N 5DU, United Kingdom; tel 020-79307932/fax 020-79309015; e-mail mtpb.london@tourism.gov.my

USA
Malaysia Tourist Information Centre, 818 Suite 804, West Seventh Street, Los Angeles, CA 90017, USA; tel 213–6899702/fax 213–6891530; e-mail malinfo@aol.com; www.visitmalaysia.com/malaysia

transport can save a lot of time. Most flights have the standard 20kg (44 pounds) checked baggage limit, although for flights on small aircraft to the islands the limit is only 10kg (22 pounds). In **Sabah** the road system is not as good as in Peninsular Malaysia, and in some areas it is better to fly; here again the cost of flying is relatively modest. There are regular ferry services to **Labuan. Sarawak** is rather different: most internal transport is by river. It is, however, now possible to fly to the cave systems commonly visited by tourists.

Singapore

By air: Singapore's Changi International Airport – 20km (12^1/$_2$ miles) from the city centre – is a major international and regional hub and is served by about 45 airlines. There are also air connections to the more popular tourist islands off Peninsular Malaysia. **By rail:** Trains from Bangkok run down the main Malaysian west-coast line to reach Singapore. **By road:** Long-distance express buses link Singapore with major towns and cities in Malaysia. **By sea:** There are regular ferries between Singapore and Indonesia's Riau archipelago. There are cruise-ship connections from Singapore to other nations.

ENTRY FORMALITIES
Your passport should be valid for at least six months from your date of entry into Singapore.

Visas
Visas are not required for citizens of Commonwealth countries, the USA and Western Europe. Citizens of these countries arriving by air receive a one-month visitors' permit on entry; those arriving by sea or from Peninsular Malaysia via the causeway receive a two-week visitors' permit. Citizens of most other countries do not require a visa for a stay of up to 14 days so long as they have confirmed onward reservations. However, citizens of China, the Commonwealth of Independent States and India must obtain a visa before arrival. If in any doubt, check with the nearest Singapore Embassy before departure.

Customs
Singapore is a free port. There is an allowance of 1 litre of liquor and 1 litre of wine. Cosmetics do not attract duty, but there is no duty-free allowance for tobacco. There are no limits on the import or export of currency. However, export permits are required for arms, ammunition, explosives, animals and plants, gold, platinum, precious stones, jewellery, poisons and drugs. You are not allowed to bring in weapons or pornography, and since 1992 the importation and sale of chewing gum has been banned. Trafficking in illegal drugs carries the death penalty. There is no duty-free allowance for goods brought in from Malaysia, and you are not entitled to duty-free goods if you have been out of Singapore for less than 48hrs.

MONEY
The unit of Singaporean currency is the Singapore dollar, usually written as $. There are 100 cents to the Singapore dollar. The Singapore dollar is directly interchangeable with the Brunei dollar and used to be so with the Malaysian ringgit, but is now worth more. When I was here in 1993 I found I could get a relatively better rate of exchange for pounds sterling than for US dollars. All major credit cards are accepted. Despite Singapore's reputation as a

place for cheap shopping – the camera shops tend to be full of Japanese tourists buying Japanese cameras – in general it is much more expensive than Malaysia. As for those consumer goods, I found that most of the items I looked at were not particularly cheap, although hard bargaining could be used to reduce prices a bit.

ACCOMMODATION

Singapore has numerous hotels ranging from luxury establishments, including some of the world's best hotels, through to low-budget guest houses. For suggestions on where to stay, refer to the Singapore Regional Directory on page 154.

ELECTRICITY

The electricity supply is 220-240 volts/50 cycles, as used in Europe, and the electrical sockets are almost always of the UK three-square-pin type, only some of the older buildings still having the two-round-pin variety. The 'token' system for governing the use of electricity in hotel rooms, as employed in Malaysia, operates here in Singapore as well.

GETTING AROUND

Singapore has an excellent internal road system. Traffic jams are kept to a minimum by strict control over car ownership and by traffic no-go areas. These inconveniences are compensated for by cheap, efficient public transport. Double- and single-decker buses charge a low fixed price. Taxis are relatively inexpensive, too, even to and from the airport, and the MRT (Mass Rapid Transport – a light railway system of which about one-third is underground) is both cheap and easy to use. In fact, if you find accommodation in the central area of the city, most of the sights of interest and the main shopping area are within walking distance.

SINGAPORE TOURIST OFFICES

For further details on other offices contact the Head Office (address below)

Head Office
Singapore Tourism Board, Tourism Court, 1 Orchard Spring Lane, Singapore 247729; tel 8313858/fax 7344456; e-mail stb_sog@stb.gov.sg; www.travel.com.sg

Overseas Offices
Australia
Singapore Tourism Board, Level 11, AWA Building, 47 York Street, Sydney NSW 2000, Australia; tel 02-92902888/fax 02-92902555

Germany
Singapore Tourism Board, Hochstrasse 35-37, 60313 Frankfurt, Germany; tel 069-9207700/fax 069-2978922

Hong Kong
Singapore Tourism Board, Room 2003 Central Plaza, 18 Harbour Road, Wanchai, Hong Kong; tel 25989290/fax 25981040

UK
1st Floor, Carrington House 126–130 Regent Street London W1R 5FE
tel 020-7437003, toll-free tel 08080 656565 (in UK only)/fax 020 77342191; www.travel.com.sg/sog

USA
NBR 12th Floor, 590 Fifth Ave, New York, NY 10036; tel 212–3024861/fax 212-3024801; e-mail kknustb@aol.com; www.singapore-usa.com
and
Suite 510, 8484 Wilshire Blvd, Beverly Hills, Los Angeles, CA 90211; tel 213–8521901/fax 323-8520129; www.singapore-usa.comz
and
Two Prudential Plaza, 180 North Stetson Avenue, Suite 2615, Chicago, Illinois 60601; tel 312-9381888/fax 312-9380086; www.singapore-usa.com

Learning to Dive

Anyone who is reasonably fit can learn to dive, and there is no better place to do it than in the tropics, where the waters are warm and where, of course, the beauty of the underwater world is likely instantly to make you a devotee for life! There are plenty of facilities offering courses in Malaysia and Singapore.

It's perfectly feasible to walk up to a beach-front dive-shop in nothing but your swimsuit and start on a diving course: everything you need can be supplied. However, as previously mentioned, many people like to buy their own kit – mask, snorkel and fins – which they can take with them anywhere. A wetsuit is another handy item to own since, although in the warm waters of the tropics you don't always need one for comfort, your wetsuit protects you from cuts and grazes and from the stings of marine organisms. If you hope to operate from a live-aboard in a remote area you will probably need to possess everything except tanks and weight belts; make sure to check with the boat operator beforehand.

The main training agencies to look for are PADI (Professional Association of Diving Instructors), BSAC (British Sub-Aqua Club), whose branches in other parts of the world include several in Malaysia, CMAS (World Underwater Federation), NAUI (National Association of Underwater Instructors) and SSI (Scuba Schools International).

Steer clear of two-tank operations working out of a beach shack. If someone approaches you on the beach and suggests you go diving, check their credentials. If the person is well qualified, fine; if not, don't go. If they are unhappy about your checking their credentials, assume the worst.

QUALIFICATIONS

In some places you will be offered a 'resort course'. This does not lead to a diving qualification but it does allow you to go underwater with an instructor to see whether or not you want to take up the sport for the longer term.

The main qualification to aim for at the start is Open-Water Certification. This usually involves five or six days' intensive training – classroom work (covering the theory and practice of diving, medical and safety procedures, etc.), pool work, some shallow dives – followed by a number of qualifying dives at sea.

Some agencies (e.g., PADI) also offer what are known as 'referral courses'. These involve learning the basics in your home country – five classroom sessions, five pool sessions – and then completing your qualifying dives on arrival at your destination. The advantage of this system is that you need spend only the first two days of your holiday under instruction and are thereafter free to enjoy the rest of it simply diving.

Once you have passed your tests you will be issued with a 'C' card from one of the regulatory bodies. This is the diver's equivalent of a driving licence and permits you, anywhere in the world, to hire tanks and go diving – always, for safety reasons, with a companion (your 'buddy'). Your Open-Water Certification successfully acquired, you can train for higher qualifications: Advanced Open-Water, Rescue Diving, Divemaster and beyond. Alternatively, you might opt to aim for special certifications such as Wreck Diver or Cave Diver.

HAZARDS

Diving is a safe sport so long as divers are thoroughly trained and they follow the time and depth tables correctly.

Never contemplate taking a diving course without having had a medical check-up, either before leaving home or on arrival in the country. Among conditions that preclude your taking up diving are epilepsy, heart disease, chest complaints, bronchitis, asthma and chronic ear and sinus problems. Don't deceive yourself into thinking 'it'll probably be all right'; it quite possibly won't be.

Flying after diving carries significant hazards. Once you have surfaced after a dive it takes several hours for the residual nitrogen in your body to disperse; were you to get straight onto a plane the low pressure inside the aircraft could cause this residual nitrogen to emerge as bubbles in your bloodstream, causing decompression sickness (the bends – see page 169). Accordingly, reputable dive operators will not permit you to dive on a day on which you plan to fly. You should always leave a gap of at least 12hr between diving and flying; a 24hr interval, if practicable, is even better.

INSURANCE

Most holiday insurance policies exclude sports such as scuba diving. It is vital that you are properly insured, since a serious incident (although they rarely happen) could involve huge costs flying you at low altitude to the nearest hospital or recompression chamber.

RESCUE LOCATION

When drift-diving, carry an inflatable 2m (7ft) rescue-location tube, so that the chase boat can find you more easily. These can be tricky to inflate and raise properly in choppy conditions, so practise first in calm waters. Tie a weight to the tube's base so that it stays upright in the water.

SPECIAL MASKS

- People with eyesight problems can have masks fitted with special corrective lenses. Your local dive-shop should be able to advise you on this.
- Low-volume masks are ideal for travelling. Not only do they take up less room but, in use, the lower volume of air inside them means they are more easily cleared of water.

RECOMPRESSION (HYPERBARIC) CHAMBERS

Recompression chambers are rare in this part of the world and as elsewhere are mostly owned and operated by the relevant navy. The Malaysian Navy has hyperbaric facilities in Lumut and Labuan, the Singapore Navy has them in Singapore while Borneo Divers have a two-man chamber in Sipadan.

Although the emergency contact numbers of these chambers are listed in full below, in practice it is always wise to ask the operator that you are diving with to approach the chamber facility on your behalf – he or she should know the correct

procedure and be able to sort out any language facilities that may prove necessary.

Labuan
Pejabit Selam, Markas Wilayah Laut Dua, 87007 Labuan F. T.; tel 087-412122 (ext. 2240)

Lamut
Department of Diving and Hyperbaric Medicine, Armed Forces Hospital, Lumut Naval Base, 32100 Lumut, Perak; tel 05-6837090 (ext. 4081)/emergencies: 05-9304023 (or the above tel number)/fax

05-6837169; e-mail ctlee@tm.net.my; www.1388.com/tldm/ hyperbaric.htm. Three-compartment Drass Galleazzi 14-person chamber.

Singapore
Naval Medicine and Hyperbaric Centre, Office of Chief Navy Medical Officer, Republic of Singapore Navy, AFPN 6060 Sembawang Camp, Admiralty Road West, Singapore 759960; tel (65) 7505544/fax (65) 7505610. Three multiple-occupancy hyperbaric chambers and two single-occupancy hyperbaric chambers.

Learning to Snorkel

It takes only a few minutes to learn to snorkel. Once you have mastered the basic techniques the way is open to hours of pleasure floating silently over the reefs watching the many fascinating creatures that live there.

Snorkelling is often considered an inferior alternative to scuba diving, but this is a misconception – for several reasons:

- Although scuba allows you to explore deep reefs, there is an enormous amount of colour on life on shallow reefs that can be appreciated just as well from the surface.
- Once you have bought your equipment, snorkelling costs nothing and is easy to organize. You can jump in wherever you want and as often as you like without having to hire tanks or make sure you have a buddy to dive with. Your time in the water isn't limited by your air supply, and you don't have to worry about the dangers of breathing compressed air at depth.
- You can often get closer to marine life if you aren't accompanied by a noisy stream of bubbles.
- Some people, for psychological, physiological or other reasons, just never take to scuba diving. If you're one of them, snorkelling could be the answer.

GETTING STARTED

Try out your gear in a swimming pool if you don't feel confident about plunging straight into the sea.

- Make sure stray hairs don't get caught under the fringe of your mask. Unless the edge is flush against your skin the mask will leak.
- Avoid overtightening the mask strap, it can give you a headache.
- Misting of the mask can be prevented by rubbing saliva on the inside of the faceplate and

---

DIVING FOR THE DISABLED

Aside from the conditions mentioned above, physical disability presents no barrier to learning to dive. In the UK the best source of information is Sub-Aqua for the Disabled, available through:

BS-AC
Telford's Quay, Ellesmere Port, South Wirral, Cheshire L65 4FY; tel 0151-3506200/fax 0151-3506215; e-mail postmaster@bsac.com; www.bsac.com

A new database called DOLPHIN (Diving Organizations Link with the Physically Handicapped and Instructors Network) aims to put suitably qualified instructors in touch with disabled divers and would-be divers. It can be contacted through:

Diving Diseases Research Centre
(The Hyperbaric Medical Centre), Tamar Science Park, Derriford Road, Plymouth, Devon, PL6 8BQ; tel 01752-209999; e-mail enquiries@ddrc.org; www.ddrc.org/ bridgedsite/contacts.htm

In the USA the main agency is:

Handicapped Scuba Association (HSA) International
1104 El Prado, San Clemente, CA 92672; tel 949-49845408; fax 949-4986128; e-mail info@hsascuba.com; www.hsascuba.com

HSA Headquarters United Kingdom & Ireland: 2A Zig Zag Road, Wallasey - Wirral, Merseyside, UK; tel/fax 0151 6302002; e-mail info@hsa-international.co.uk; www.hsa-international.co.uk

---

DIVE FACILITIES IN KUALA LUMPUR

There are various dive facilities in Kuala Lumpur; the following is a selection:

Asian Overland Services 39C & 40C, Jalan Memanda 9, Ampang Point, Taman Dato Ahmad Razali, 68000 Ampang, Selangor Darul Ehsan; tel 03-4529100; e-mail aos@aostt.po.my
Borneo Divers and Sea Sports (KL) 127,

Jalan 21/37, 47400 Damansara Utama; tel 03-7173066; e-mail bdsskl@po.jaring.my. PADI 5-star IDC Centre and Underwater.
Global Scuba 34, Jln. SS1518 Subang Jaya, 47500 Petaling Jaya, Selangor; tel 603-03-735 5167/fax 603-03-735 0823
Pro Dive 23 Jalan Dang Wangi, 50100 KL; tel 03-2929072/fax 03-2929317

Richmond Supplies & Services (Dive Centre) Utama 47800, Selangor; tel 03-77269932; e-mail rmond@dingnet.com.sg
Scuba Quest Lot 3-38, 2nd Floor, Wisma Central, Jalan Ampany, 50450 KL; tel 03-2642697; e-mail info@scuba-quest.com.my
Scuba Station 48, Jalan SS22/21 Damansara Jaya, 47400 Petaling Jaya; tel 03-7161616; e-mail scubast@po.jaring.my

then rinsing with sea water. There are anti-misting products on the market which have the same effect, but saliva is readily available and free.
- If water gets into your mask, simply put your head above the surface and apply pressure to the top rim. The water will run out of the bottom.
- To clear the snorkel of water, put your head above the surface, tilt your head back and exhale vigorously. Always take the next breath slowly, since there may still be a little water left in the snorkel. Another strong blow and your snorkel should be clear.

MOVING THROUGH THE WATER

A lot of nonsense is written about the correct way to fin. The 'approved' method is to keep your legs straight, since this gives maximum efficiency; the 'wrong' way is to bicycle with your legs – i.e., to draw your knees in before you kick out. However, although the 'wrong' way may be slightly less efficient, what does it matter? The important things are that you are comfortable and going where you want to go.

Similarly, snorkelling manuals generally tell you not to use your hands and arms for propulsion. Although this is good advice for divers – novices are easily recognized by their flapping arms – for snorkellers it is basically irrelevant. Beneath the surface you may want to supplement straight fin-kicking with breast-stroke in order to increase your range, while the fastest way to travel on the surface is to use the crawl.

FREE DIVING

The term 'free diving' is sometimes used to describe snorkelling in general. In fact, what it means is diving beneath the surface without scuba tanks. Anyone who is fit can, with sufficient practice, reach depths of 7–9m (20–30ft) in the tropics. Local people often go to depths of 21m (70ft) when collecting pearls and the like.

The most important point to remember when free diving is to equalize the pressure in your ears as you descend. Sometimes they equalize of their own accord. Failing this, simply hold the nosepiece of your mask and blow gently through your nose; this should make your ears 'pop' themselves clear. If your ears hurt it's because they haven't cleared properly – an effect that can be exacerbated by a cold or bad sinuses. Come up and try again: do not continue to descend on the assumption that your ears will clear sooner or later.

As you go deeper you may feel pressure building up and pushing your mask into your face. To alleviate this, simply exhale gently through your nose.

The best way to go under the surface is to use a duck dive (surface dive). Bend forward at the waist and lift your legs perpendicular to the surface. The weight of your legs should now cause you to sink until your fins are below the surface. If necessary, augment the dive with a couple of breast-strokes.

In order to stay underwater longer you can – at your own risk – use hyperventilation. This involves inhaling and exhaling very deeply several times before you dive. The hazard is that hyperventilation can lead to sudden unconsciousness underwater or even after you have resurfaced and taken another breath. Snorkelling manuals counsel against it, but most snorkellers try it at one time or another and some do it all the time. Because of the dangers the practice can hardly be recommended. However, if you do try it – perhaps at the instigation of more experienced companions – take precautions to make it as safe as possible. Never exceed four hyperventilations before a dive. After the dive, rest on the surface for at least a couple of minutes before hyperventilating again. Never hyperventilate when diving on your own.

A last point about free diving which is often forgotten. As you surface, look upwards. Otherwise you might crash into a boat or someone swimming on the surface!

3 PULAU SEGANTANG

★★

Location: West of the southern end of Pulau Payar.
Access: By boat from wherever you are based.
Conditions: Can be rougher than the other sites in this area, so it is best to dive only when the conditions are calm.
Average depth: 20m (65ft)
Maximum depth: 30m (100ft)

Pulau Segantang comprises two steep-sided jagged rocky outcrops which join up underwater; they continue down to muddy sand at 20m (65ft).

In the deeper waters there are gorgonian sea fans growing on the walls and yellow *Tubastrea* cup corals under overhangs; soft corals swell up whenever the current plays across them. Sea anemones with attendant clownfish cluster in any relatively flat area.

The fish life is good, from shoals of juveniles to giant groupers, with many species of angelfish, butterflyfish, lionfish, scorpionfish, stonefish, jacks, rainbow runners, tuna, fusiliers, snappers, garfish, pufferfish, moray eels, whitetip reef sharks, leopard (Variegated) sharks and giant stingrays. The two outcrops also attract pelagic species, including whale sharks. Nudibranchs are common, and you can still find murex shells, ghost pipefish and spiny lobsters.

Some boats impounded for illegal fishing have been sunk off Pulau Payar. Their wrecks make good diving, although you must obtain permission from the marine-park staff.

Above: *The Yellowmask Angelfish (Pomacanthus xanthometopon), also known as the Blue-face Angelfish, is one of many angelfish whose juveniles have totally different colour patterns.*

How to Get There

Langkawi and Pulau Pinang are serviced by regular international and domestic flights. There are some ferries to Langkawi from Thailand, and ferries run three days a week from Pulau Pinang and regularly from Kuala Kedah (1hr) and Kuala Perlis (45min). You can travel by road from Kuala Lumpur to Kuala Kedah via Alor Setar (474km; 294 miles) or Kuala Perlis (524km; 323 miles). There are also rail connections from Kuala Lumpur and Singapore to Alor Setar.

Pulau Pinang has connections with Singapore, Kuala Lumpur and Thailand by rail; from Kuala Lumpur by road is 380km (234 miles). There are very frequent ferries from Butterworth (15min), or you can cross by the Penang Bridge (toll).

A boat direct from Kuala Kedah to Pulau Payar takes 1hr and a boat from Pulau Pinang to Pulau Payar takes 4hr.

There are regular ferry services from Lumut to both Pulau Pangkor and Pulau Pangkor Laut. Lumut is 170km (105 miles) south of Butterworth, 83km (52 miles) from Ipoh and 183km (114 miles) from Kuala Lumpur by road. Ipoh is serviced regularly by air and rail from Kuala Lumpur.

Permission to visit Payar Marine Park must be obtained from: **Department of Fisheries Malaysia,** Ministry of Agriculture, 8th & 9th Floor, Wisma Tani, Jalan Sultan Salahuddin, 50628 Kuala Lumpur; tel 03-2982011/fax 03-2910305; or from **Wisma Persekutuan** Jalan Kampung Bharu, 05000 Alor Setar; tel 04-7342135/fax 04-7304623; e-mail perikanan@tm.net.my

Where to Stay

Langkawi
Luxury
Radisson Tanjung Rhu Mukim Ayer Hangat, 07000 Langkawi; tel 04-9591083/fax 04-9591899; e-mail resort@tanjungrhu.com.my web site http://www.tanjungrhu.com.my. Luxurious resort covering a large area and offering a range of non-motorized water sports.

Upper Price Range
Pelangi Beach Resort Pantai Cenang, 07000 Langkawi; tel 04–9551001/fax 04–9551122; e-mail pelangi.pbl@meritus-hotels.com; www.meritus-hotels.com.sg/malaysia/pelangi. Luxurious ethnic wooden chalets based on traditional architecture, most recreational facilities, children especially welcome.

Langkawi Island Resort Jalan Pantai Dato Syed Omar, Kuah; tel 04–9666209/fax 04- 9666414

Lower Price Range
Hotel Langkasuka Batu 3/4, A–14–15, Pokok Asam Kuah, 07000 Langkawi; tel 04-9666571/fax 04-9661371. Good accommodation at a lower price.

Outside Kuah
Langkawi Chalet 1 Kampung Penarak

Kuah, 07000 Langkawi; tel 05-9667993/fax 04-9660680. Good accommodation at a lower price.

Pantai Cenang
Sandy Beach Motel Pantai Cenang, 07000 Langkawi; tel 04-9551308/fax 04-9551762. Good accommodation at a lower price.

Pantai Tengah
Federal Lodge Lot 1698 Pantai Tengah; tel 04-9551701/fax 04-9551504; e-mail lhvok@tm.net.my; www.hijau.com.my/holidayvilla. All quality facilities.

Pulau Pinang
Upper Price Range
Eastern & Oriental Hotel 10 Farquhar Street, 10200 Pulau Pinang; tel 04-2630630/fax 04-2634833

City Bay View Hotel 25A Lebuh Farquhar, Georgetown; tel 04-2633161/fax 04-2634124; e-mail cbvpg@tm.net.my. Three-star accommodation at a good price.

Ferringhi Beach Hotel Jalan Low Yat, 11000 Penang; tel 04-8905999/fax 04-8905100; e-mail ferringhi@po.jaring.my; www.interconti.com. Four-star accommodation at a good price.

Shangri-La Jalan Magazine, 10300 Penang; tel 04-2622622/fax 04-2615967; e-mail slp@shangri-la.com; www.shangri-la.com:80/shangri-la/hotels/21/21home.html. Top class accommodation – there are other Shangri-La hotels in the area.

Lower Price Range
YMCA 211-B Jalan Macalister, 10450 Penang; tel 04-2288211. Clean accommodation at rock-bottom prices.

Hotel Agora 202A Jalan Macalister, 10400 Pulau Pinang; tel 04-2298588/fax 04-2265959

Pulau Pangkor Laut
Pulau Pangkor Laut Resort tel 05-6991100/fax 05-6991200. All luxurious facilities, choice of accommodation on land or over water.

Dive facilities

Dive clubs and dive training agencies sometimes organize boats to Pulau Payar from Pulau Pinang. The only permanent diving facilities are at a few resorts on Langkawi.

Asian Overland Services, 33M Jalan Dewan Sultan Sulaiman 1 (off Jalan Tunku Abdul Rahman), 50300 Kuala Lumpur; tel 03–2925622/fax 03–2925209

Blue Marlin Dive Centre Penang, Tanjong Tokong Road, 10350 Penang; tel 020-4361932

The China Emporium (Hobi-Sports) 234, Ground Floor, Penang Road, 10000 Penang; tel 04-2642171/fax 04-2643125. Retail outlet.

Langkawi Coral Langkawi Saga Travel & Tours Sdn. Bhd., Jalan Sungai Emas, Batu Ferringhi, 11100 Penang; tel 04-8812250/fax 04-8812252

Langkawi Island Resort Jalan Pantai Dato Syed Omar, Kuah; tel 04-9666209/fax 04-9666414. Luxury accommodation.

Langkawi Saga Travel & Tours Sdn. Bhd. 10 Taman Seri Negeri, Jalan Penarak, 07000 Langkawi; tel 04-9669140. A 50-minute cruise on a luxury catamaran to Payar Marine Park.

Oceanquest Malaysia 11 Bangunan MDL, Jin Persiaran Putra Kuah, 07000 Langkawi; tel 020-49667379

Pangkor Laut Resort Pulau Pangkor Laut; tel 05-6991100/fax 05-6991200

Pelangi Beach Resort Pantai Cenang, 07000 Langkawi; tel 04-9551001/fax 04-9551122; e-mail pelangi.pbl@meritus-hotels.com; www.meritus-hotels.com.sg/malaysia/pelangi. Luxurious ethnic wooden chalets based on traditional architecture.

Pro Dive Lot 974, Pantai Cenang, 07000 Langkawi; tel 04-9553739/fax 04–955 3475 (A branch of Pro Dive in Kuala Lumpur) PADI 5-star Instructor Development Centre

Pro Dive 18 Jalan Pakawali, 11200 Hillside Penang; tel 026-48903919. PADI 5-star Instructor Development Centre.

Sriwani Tours & Travel Sdn. Bhd. Lot 1-21, Jetty Point Complex, 07000 Langkawi; tel 04-9667318/fax 04-9667308; e-mail dakhoos@pc.jaring.my; www.sriwani.com.my

Film Processing

None is available on the islands. For Payar, the nearest processing on the mainland is by:

Star Colour Sdn Bhd, 24 Jalan Petani, 08000 Sungai Petani, Kedah; tel 04–425895

President Foto, 4114 Jalan Bagan Luar, Butterworth; tel 04–318601

For Pangkor and the Sembilan Islands, use Kuala Lumpur suppliers (see listing on page 19) or:

Photo Speed Corporation Sdn Bhd, 90–92 Jalan Sultan Idris Shah, 30000 Ipoh; tel 05–532006/fax 05–501217

Hospitals

Payar
District Hospital, Langkawi; tel 04–196422

General Hospital, Alor Setar; tel 04–723333

General Hospital, Pulau Pinang, Jalan Residensi; tel 04–373333

Pangkor and the Sembilan Islands
Ipoh District Hospital, tel 05–533333

Lumut District Hospital, tel 05–935333

Kuala Lumpur General Hospital, Jalan
Pahang; tel 03–2921044

LOCAL HIGHLIGHTS

Langkawi
The resorts here have everything from golf to
horse-riding, not to mention jungle and hill
trekking, bird-watching and walks along which
you can search out butterflies and tropical
flowers. Pulau Singa Besar has been turned
into a wildlife sanctuary and marine reserve.
Pulau Pinang (Penang)
Pulau Pinang is the pearl of the Orient. Its lure
goes beyond its palm-fringed beaches to the
elegant colonial buildings and the rich variety
of ethnic cultures represented here.

Among the many sights are the **Kek Lok Si
Temple**, the **Pinang State Mosque** and the
Moorish architecture of the **Kapitan Keling
Mosque** and the **Kuan Yin Teng Temple**
(1800), the oldest temple in Pulau Pinang. **Wat
Chayamankalaram** has a reclining Buddha
33m (108ft) long. **Khoo Konsi Temple** is
Pulau Pinang's most picturesque building. **The
Snake Temple** was built in 1850 in memory of
the Buddhist priest Chor Soo Kong; it contains,
as the name might suggest, a variety of snakes.
The oldest Hindu temple on Pulau Pinang is the
Sri Mariamman Temple (1833); the biggest is
Nattukotai Chettiar Temple on Waterfall
Road. Also of interest is the **Bat Temple** at Air
Itam. Relics of the British presence include Fort
Cornwallis, dating from 1804–5, and St
George's Anglican Church, built in 1818.

There is a **butterfly farm** at Teluk Bahang
and the orchid and hibiscus garden on Bukit

Jambul is worth a visit, as are the museum and
art galleries. You can take a trip up Pinang Hill
on the funicular railway; there are services every
30min. **The Pinang Bridge** is worth seeing.

West Coast Mainland
On the mainland, a short ferry-ride away, is
Kedah. This state is Malaysia's ricebowl. There
are many historical buildings in and around
Alor Setar, including the **Zahir Mosque** and,
opposite the mosque, the Thai-influenced
Balai Besar ('Great Hall'), built in 1898 and
used for royal and state occasions. **The Balai
Nobat** ('music hall') houses the sacred instru-
ments of the royal orchestra.

At Langgar are the **Royal Mausoleum**,
the **Royal Boat House** (facing Darulaman
Stadium on the banks of the Sungai Anak
Bukit), the **Di Raja State Museum** and the
Balai Seni Negeri (the state art gallery).
Pekan Rabu Bazaar sells traditional goods
and handicrafts of the Kedah region.

If you have the energy you could try a
climb up **Gunung Jerai** (Kedah Peak), which
is 1200m (3937ft) high; on and around the
mountain are paths, waterfalls and campsites.

Between Gunung Jerai in the north and
Sungai Muda in the south is **Lembah Bujang**,
Malaysia's richest archaeological area. Here
there are Indian temples believed to date from
the 5th century; 50 have been discovered, of
which eight have so far been restored.

Pulau Pangkor and Pulau Pangkor Laut
Pulau Pangkor and Pulau Pangkor Laut are oriented towards beach-resort activities, notably
watersports. Pulau Pangkor has Indian and
Chinese temples as well as the Dutch Fort
(built 1670) at Teluk Gedan.

Perak is called the 'silver state' because of
the wealth it has derived from the mining of

> ## HISTORIC SITES ON LANGKAWI
>
> Most of the sites you can visit on
> Langkawi are associated with Malaysian
> folklore. They include:
> - **Makam Mahsuri**, the tomb of
>   Princess Mahsuri
> - **Padang Matsirat**, the Field of
>   Burnt Rice
> - **Telaga Tujuh**, the Seven Pools
> - **Telaga Air Hangat**, the Hot Spring
> - **Pasir Hitam**, the Beach of Black
>   Sand
> - **Tasik Dayang Bunting**, the Lake of
>   the Pregnant Maiden
> - **Gua Langsir**, the Cave of the
>   Banshee, 91m (300ft) high, where
>   thousands of bats roost
> Other attractions include Pantai Rhu – a
> beach named after the shady *Casuarina*
> trees – and the waterfall at Durian
> Perangin.

not silver but tin. It has the imposing,
Moorish-style railway station at Ipoh, Buddhist
cave temples, the Tambun hot springs, the
Ubudiah Mosque, the Sam Poh Tong Temple,
the Perak Museum, the leaning tower at Teluk
Intan and the unfinished Kellie's Castle.

The Cameron Highlands are 60km (37
miles) off the Kuala Lumpur–
Ipoh–Butterworth road.

*The tiny, privately owned, island of
Pangkor Laut boasts a luxury resort
offering diving and water sports.*

Night on a coral reef is a time of change. Many diurnal fish alter their colours at night. Sometimes the change is minor, but in other cases it can be total; occasionally it is similar to that used by the same fish at a cleaning station to signal it is ready for cleaning. In some instances solid colours become blotchy, while on other fish bold patterns appear; the effect in either event is to make the fish more difficult for predators to pick out against the background.

Dusk and dawn are the times when predators are at their most active, rising unseen out of the darkness to take prey silhouetted against the still light sky. One can often sit on a boat or jetty in the evening watching the water churn as shoals of small fish are attacked by jacks, tuna or barracuda. There really is no escape for the unfortunate victims: if they jump out of the water to escape the predators from beneath they are likely to be snapped up by the sea birds hovering expectantly overhead.

Bumphead Parrotfish (Bolbometopon muricatum) asleep in a cave at night. Parrotfish often change colour or encase themselves in a cocoon to discourage predators.

NIGHTLIFE

Diving at night is a fascinating experience, as one's light picks out small fishes and other creatures adopting their different stratagems to avoid the attentions of larger ones. Parrotfish and butterflyfish hide in crevices in the reef and angelfish penetrate even further, either concealing themselves completely or leaving just an eye or snout in view. Most wrasse bury themselves in the sand, as do some pufferfish, lizardfish, flounders and rays – not that this is a foolproof tactic, as many sharks have electro-receptors that can detect the hidden fish. Snappers and grunts shoal in small, closely knit groups in caves, small valleys or between gorgonians. Triggerfish flatten themselves against depressions in the coral; smaller Hawksbill and Green Turtles do likewise if they cannot find a cave or a large enough gorgonian to use for concealment. Every nook and cranny in the coral contains something of interest: shrimps, prawns, crabs, lobsters, cuttlefish, worms, octopuses ...

A BLAZE OF COLOUR

However, not all of the denizens of the reef are elusive at night. Various fish – like squirrelfish, soldierfish, bigeyes and cardinalfish – feed at night, and some less common fish can

be seen only at night. Nudibranchs, sea urchins, flat worms, cowries, conches, huge tun shells and sea cucumbers come out to graze. Overhanging roofs are turned into a blaze of colour by the feeding polyps of *Tubastrea* corals. Sea hares graze sedately, ready to eject a spurt of magenta ink if anything touches them. Moray eels dash from crevice to crevice. Clownfish, shut out because the anemones that are their daytime homes are closed for the night, lurk forlornly. Comb jellies, often too transparent to be easily noticed in daylight, show clearly in your torchlight. Young cuttlefish and shellfish hide among the long spines of spiny urchins. Meanwhile, small crabs and brittle stars feed among the arms of corals and gorgonians.

TORCHLIGHT

The shallows are the realm of basket stars, brittle stars and feather stars, which sift the current for plankton. If your light is too bright these creatures will curl up and disappear too quickly for you to see them, so keep your torchlight level low. Other reactions to torchlight differ: diurnal fishes, hiding in holes or acting sleepily over the reef at night, are often mesmerized by lights, so that you can come

---

NIGHTLIFE

Before you leave the water, turn off your light for a few minutes. At first it will be all the noise that surprises you: creatures eating, snapping and grunting. However, as your eyes get used to the dark, you will start noticing many phosphorescent creatures. Notable among these will be Flashlight Fish, *Photoblepharon*, swimming around in small shoals; a pouch beneath each eye contains bioluminescent algae, so that the area glows like a firefly. Also evident will be phosphorescent plankton: if you wave your arms about you will disturb millions of these, so that it will be as if you were in the midst of a snowstorm of light.

---

up very close to them; many will spread out their fins to look larger in an attempt to frighten you off, and some pufferfish will inflate. Particularly interesting are the larger parrotfish, which at night back into unlikely-looking overhangs, holes or branched corals and fall asleep. Their eyes remain open, but the fishes ignore lights and can be stroked. If you are diving very late you can find them enclosed in a cocoon of mucus, believed to act as a protection against predators and parasites.

Flat worms (Pseudoceros sp.) crawl across the reef at night and are rarely seen in the day.

5 TERUMBU TIGA (TIGER ROCKS)

★★★★

Location: Just south of Pasir Tinggi, at the centre of the east coast of Pulau Perhentian Besar.

Access: By boat (55min) from the resort clockwise around Pulau Perhentian Besar.

Conditions: Can be rough, with a strong current and swell after a heavy storm; novices should dive here only in calm weather. Visibility is about 10m (33ft) on average.

Average depth: 10m (33ft)

Maximum depth: 20m (65ft)

This dive is claimed to be the best off the Perhentian Islands. I did it twice. In both instances it was as a drift-dive in bad weather, with a heavy swell and less than 2m (6ft) visibility, but I still found it very good. If the visibility had been better I would have given it five stars rather than four. The site is the usual jumble of large boulders down to sand, but is teeming with fish and, when a current is running, has some of the biggest soft corals I have seen anywhere. The shallow rocks are carpeted with leathery soft corals and purple *Dendronephthya* soft tree corals, while down around the 9m (30ft) mark are good *Acropora* table corals, cup corals and zoanthids.

The deeper rocks have fluted oysters and lots of large white gorgonian sea fans, weighed down with wing oysters; there are also many red harp corals and green *Tubastrea micranthus* corals, some with their polyps out feeding during the day. Down on the sand are huge *Dendronephthya rubeola* soft tree corals, some black corals, small whip corals, many varieties of sea cucumbers, sea stars, cushion stars and various shells (including cowrie and volute shells) and nudibranchs. Barrel sponges covered with Alabaster Sea Cucumbers are most noticeable.

The fish life includes barracuda, batfish, surgeonfish, lionfish, scorpionfish, filefish, angelfish, butterflyfish, parrotfish, Coral Trout (and other groupers), moray eels, snappers, sweetlips, Whitecheek Monocle Bream, Threadfin Bream, razorfish, hawkfish, Bumphead Parrotfish and shoals of jacks, parrotfish and fusiliers. There are feather stars everywhere plus the occasional turtle. Sadly, there is also a working fish trap.

6 BATU BUTUK   7 TANJUNG TUKAS

★★★

Location: The southeast corner of Pulau Perhentian Besar.

Access: By boat (30min) from the resort anticlockwise around Pulau Perhentian Besar.

Conditions: Usually calm; can be choppy with a current in bad weather. The average visibility is about 7m (23ft).

Average depth: 12m (40ft)

Maximum depth: 18m (60ft)

A jumble of boulders descending to sand, with good stony corals but fewer soft corals than at Terumbu Tiga (Site 5). Likewise, the fish and shellfish life is similar but less prolific. Turtles are sometimes found on the west side of Tanjung Tukas.

8 TELUK DALAM

★★★★

Location: The west side of the main southern bay of Pulau Perhentian Besar.

Access: By boat (20min) from the resort anticlockwise around Pulau Perhentian Besar.

Conditions: Usually calm – good protection from the weather. Visibility only about 7m (23ft) on average.

Average depth: 9m (30ft)

Maximum depth: 15m (50ft)

A jumble of rocks going down to sand. The deeper rocks support many black corals, and these in turn support many wing oysters. On the sand you can find many sea anemones, sea cucumbers, sea urchins, sea stars, nudibranchs and shells, plus the occasional stingray.

9 GUA KAMBING

★★★★★★

Location: South of the Cempaka Chalets on the east coast of Pulau Perhentian Kecil.

Access: By boat (about 20min) from the resort southwest across the channel between the two islands.

Conditions: Generally calm, although there may be a slight current. Average visibility only about 7m (23ft).

Average depth: 9m (30ft)

Maximum depth: 15m (50ft)

Yet again, this site offers a jumble of boulders going down to a sandy bottom. Usually on view are pufferfish, filefish, surgeonfish, unicornfish and parrotfish, and there are patches of stony corals with angelfish and butterflyfish. On the sand are sea stars, cushion stars, sea cucumbers, sea anemones, moray eels and stingrays.

PULAU LANG TENGAH
This resort can be reached by boat from Merang. Contact: **Blue Coral Island Resort Sales Office** 7, Lorong Yap Kwan Seng, 50450 Kuala Lumpur; tel 03-2626166/fax 03-2617628 web site http://www.strawberrypark-hotels.com
Divers tend to go to Pulau Redang or Pulau Perhentian for serious diving.

10 SHIPWRECK

★★★

Location: South–southwest of the southwest corner of Pulau Perhentian Kecil.

Access: By boat (about 30min) from the resort southwest to the southern end of Pulau Perhentian Kecil, then round to the southwest end.

Conditions: Generally calm; the surface current decreases as you descend to the wreck. Surface conditions can be bad after bad weather. The visibility is not good – only about 7m (23ft).

Average depth: 22m (72ft)

Maximum depth: 24m (80ft)

This is half of a steel landing craft which originally came to Malaysia bearing Vietnamese boat people. It was being towed back to Kuala Besut for repairs when it sunk in 1976.

The whereabouts of the other half was not known to Stephen Ng and his staff of the dive centre at Perhentian Island Resort.

This is not in fact a particularly good wreck dive, though it can be penetrated, but it is a splendid haven for marine life: big *Dendronephthya* soft tree corals and black corals covered in wing oysters and feather stars, together with all the fish you might expect in this area, including filefish, hawkfish, Pennant Coralfish and the local species of angelfish, butterflyfish, batfish, snappers, wrasse, jacks, barracuda, groupers and stingrays.

ARTIFICIAL REEFS

Constructing artificial reefs in shallow waters is, as any sea fisherman will tell you, an excellent way of enhancing fish stocks. Purpose-built artificial reefs are commonly placed either on damaged reefs or on the seabed near reefs about 1.5km (1 mile) offshore.

Artificial reefs have been laid all around Malaysia; mostly by the Department of Fisheries (31 off the east and west coasts of Johor State alone by 1994) but also by Raleigh International volunteers and by fishermen themselves. There are reef-rescue projects underway off Singapore.

Most often used for the construction are old tyres chained together, sometimes stabilized by concrete blocks. The system is cheap and highly effective, although there is a risk the tyres may release toxic pollutants as they gradually deteriorate, and the 'reef' is likely to break up when caught in a trawl net – not as uncommon an event as one might think. Concrete slabs or small pyramids chained together or linked with chain-link fencing would seem a better, if more expensive, system.

Artificial reefs need not be deliberate constructions. Shipwrecks rapidly take on the attributes of a reef, forming a good substratum for coral larvae to settle on and offering shelter for bigger fish and breeding sites for smaller fish and invertebrates.

---

11 PASIR KERANGI: PVC-PIPE ARTIFICiAL REEF

★★★★

Location: West of Pulau Perhentian Kecil, midway between Coral Bay and Mira's Place.

Access: By boat (about 45min) from the resort southwest and then around the west side of Pulau Perhentian Kecil.

Conditions: Generally slightly choppy with quite a strong surface current, which gets less as you pull down the line from the buoy. The pipe structure is open, so there is no lee. Visibility is usually only about 7m (23ft).

Average depth: 18m (60ft)

Maximum depth: 18m (60ft)

I dived this artificial reef (an open latticework of polyvinyl chloride pipes anchored down on sand in 1991) after bad weather, in a strong current and with almost zero visibility, but I was still impressed. The prolific growth on the pipes in such a short time of *Dendronephthya* soft tree corals – up to 80cm (30in) high – and of black corals, sponges and wing oysters is quite amazing.

12 PULAU SERENGGEH: SOUTH END

★★★

Location: The southern end of Pulau Serenggeh, due west from the northern end of Perhentian Pulau Kecil.

Access: By boat (about 50min) from the resort northwest around the north coast of Pulau Perhentian Kecil, then out due west to Pulau Serenggeh.

Conditions: Usually a bit choppy with some current. Visibility, generally about 10m (33ft), is better than around the two larger Perhentians.

Average depth: 12m (40ft)

Maximum depth: 18m (60ft)

This site comprises a jumble of rocks descending to sand, with small soft corals on the rocks in the shallow water, black corals, fire corals, gorgonian sea fans and harp corals on the deeper rocks, and lots of whip corals on the sand. The fish life is good.

13 TANJUNG PANGLIMA ABU

★★★★

Location: Northwest corner of Pulau Perhentian Kecil.

Access: By boat (about 40min) northwest from the resort, then the north coast of Pulau Perhentian Kecil.

Conditions: Normally calm – it is not worth diving here if the conditions are rough or choppy. Visibility is normally only about 7m (23ft).

Average depth: 12m (40ft)
Maximum depth: 15m (50ft)
A shallow dive with some big boulder corals. Novice divers and strong snorkellers would find it attractive.

14 TANJUNG BUTUNG

★★★

Location: North of the northwest corner of Pulau Perhentian Kecil.
Access: By boat (about 40min) northwest from the resort and then around the north coast of Pulau Perhentian Kecil.
Conditions: Usually calm; it can sometimes be choppy with some current. The visibility here is generally about 10m; 33ft.
Average depth: 18m (60ft)
Maximum depth: 25m (82ft)
A jumble of rocks descending to sand at 25m (80ft). The rocks sport leathery soft corals and some quite big *Dendronephthya* soft tree corals. A good variety of fish live at the site, including all the local species of angelfish and butterflyfish, batfish, filefish, parrotfish, groupers and moray eels, plus shoals of fusiliers, snappers, jacks and trevallies.

15 TOKONG LAUT

★★★★

Location: West–northwest of the northwest corner of Pulau Perhentian Kecil.
Access: By boat (about 50min) northwest from the resort, around the north coast of Pulau Perhentian Kecil, and then out to the west–northwest.

Conditions: Usually a bit choppy; can be rough after storms (I dived here in a heavy swell with a strong surge). These waters are nice and clear: expect visibility around 30m (100ft).
Average depth: 10m (33ft)
Maximum depth: 19m (62ft)
A jumble of large boulders going down to sand. In the rocks are caves and tunnels you can swim through. The upper rocks are liberally carpeted with leathery soft corals and small *Dendronephthya* soft tree corals; the deeper ones are covered in black corals, gorgonian sea fans, stinging hydroids and harp corals, together with lots of sea anemones, clownfish, zoanthids, bubble corals, wing oysters and oysters. Down on the sand there are some large barrel sponges covered in Alabaster Sea Cucumbers, many species of sea stars, cushion stars, sea cucumbers, nudibranchs and congregations of black sea urchins. Parrotfish, angelfish, butterflyfish, rabbitfish, pufferfish (many varieties), lionfish, surgeonfish, unicorn-fish, damselfish, cardinalfish, lizardfish, hawkfish and stingrays may all be seen, as well as shoals of sweetlips, snappers, razorfish and fusiliers.

16 PULAU SUSU DARA BESAR: NORTH SIDE

★★★★

Location: The north side of the larger of the two Susu Dara islets, west–northwest of the northwest corner of Pulau Perhentian Kecil.
Access: By boat (about 50min) from the resort northwest around the north coast of Pulau Perhentian Kecil and

Below: *One of the many beautiful, unspoilt beaches of Pulau Perhentian Besar, fringed by coconut palms.*

A HAVEN FOR RAPID CORAL GROWTH

The growth-rates of gorgonian sea fans, black corals, soft corals and mussels in the warm shallow waters around the Perhentians are truly remarkable.

In 1991, as an experiment for the Malaysian Fisheries Department, Stephen Ng and his assistants used corkscrew anchors to lay an artificial reef, made from PVC plastic pipes, at 18m (60ft) on the sandy bottom. Just two years later, when I dived here in October 1993, these pipes had become a haven for fish life, and were covered in soft corals and mussels; I measured several *Dendronephthya* soft-tree corals that were 70–80cm (27½–31in) tall. (For more on this, see Site 11.)

---

then out west–northwest to Pulau Susu Dara Besar.
Conditions: Usually a bit choppy; can be rough after bad weather.
Average depth: 10m (33ft)
Maximum depth: 18m (60ft)
This site offers much the same as Tokong Laut (Site 15); although the fish life is just as good and plentiful, the corals are a bit less exciting. The waters are as beautifully clear as at Tokong Laut.

17 PULAU SUSU DARA KECIL: NORTH SIDE

★★★★

Location: The north side of the smaller of the two Susu Dara islets, northeast of Pulau Susu Dara Besar.
Access: By boat (about 50min) northwest from the resort around the north coast of Pulau Perhentian Kecil and out west–northwest to Pulau Susu Dara Kecil.
Conditions: Usually a bit choppy; can be rough after bad weather.
Average depth: 10m (33ft)
Maximum depth: 18m (60ft)
Much the same as Tokong Laut (Site 15), and with the same lovely clear visibility. The fish life is just as good and plentiful, the corals not quite so good.

18 TOKONG BOPENG: NORTH SIDE

★★★★

Location: The north side of Tokong Bopeng, west–northwest of the northwest corner of Pulau Perhentian Kecil, and west of Pulau Rawa.
Access: By boat (about 50min) northwest from the resort around the north coast of Pulau Perhentian Kecil and out west–northwest to Tokong Bopeng.
Conditions: Usually a bit choppy; can be rough after bad weather.

Average depth: 10m (33ft)
Maximum depth: 18m (60ft)
Much the same as Tokong Laut (Site 15), and with the same excellent visibility: fish life just as good and plentiful, corals not quite so good.

19 TOKONG BURUNG KECIL

★★★

Location: South of Tokong Bopeng.
Access: By boat (50min) northwest from the resort around the north coast of Pulau Perhentian Kecil and then out west–northwest.
Conditions: Usually calm; can be choppy after bad weather. Average visibility about 10m (33ft).
Average depth: 9m (30ft)
Maximum depth: 15m (50ft)
A jumble of boulders descends to sand. This site is quite good for corals, but the fish life is less than brilliant.

20 PULAU RAWA: SOUTHEAST CORNER

★★★

Location: West–northwest of the northeast corner of Pulau Perhentian Kecil, east of the Pulau Susu Dara islets.
Access: By boat (about 50min) northwest from the resort around the north coast of Pulau Perhentian Kecil and out west–northwest to Pulau Rawa.
Conditions: Usually choppy; can be rough after bad weather. Visibility is about 10m (33ft) on average.
Average depth: 20m (65ft)
Maximum depth: 30m (100ft)
The site comprises a jumble of big boulders forming caves and tunnels you can swim into and through. There are some soft corals, black corals and gorgonian sea fans, but the scenery and fish life are not as good as at the other sites (Sites 15–19) in the area west–northwest of Pulau Perhentian Kecil.

21 TELUK KERMA

★★★

Location: The southern end of the headland east of D. Lagoon on the east coast of Pulau Perhentian Kecil.
Access: By boat (about 30min) west–northwest from the resort.
Conditions: Usually calm with some slight current. Visibility normally about 10m (33ft).
Average depth: 13m (43ft)
Maximum depth: 13m (43ft)
Here you find, as usual for this region, a jumble of rocks

from the coast down to the sand; you can then swim along the junction of the rocks with the sand. There are a few stony corals plus many species of pufferfish, parrotfish, surgeonfish, snappers and some Bumphead Parrotfish and turtles. On the sand you can see several species of sea cucumbers, sea stars – including Crown-of-Thorns Starfish – stingrays and sea urchins.

 ### BATU NISAN

★★★

Location: The headland north of Matahari Chalets, on the east coast of Pulau Perhentian Kecil.
Access: By boat (about 20min) just north of west from Perhentian Island Resort.
Conditions: Usually calm with some slight current. Visibility generally about 10m (33ft).
Average depth: 13m (43ft)
Maximum depth: 13m (43ft)

A jumble of rocks descends from the coast to the sand, where you are guaranteed to see stingrays, fan worms, several species of sea cucumbers and sea stars – including the Crown-of-Thorns Starfish – as well as congregations of black sea urchins. In the water over the rocks are many species, both large and small, of pufferfish, boxfish, surgeonfish, unicornfish, parrotfish, snappers, sweetlips and fusiliers.

Gorgonian Sea Fan (Subergorgia hicksoni). Sea fans usually grow on the edge of a reef where they are exposed to plankton-bearing currents. Some specimens are very large, perhaps as much as 3m (10ft) across.

How to Get There

The cheapest way to reach Perhentian from Europe is to fly with Malaysian Airlines via Kuala Lumpur to either Kota Bharu or Kuala Terengganu; then take either a bus (very cheap) or taxi (cheap) to Kuala Besut. From Kuala Besut there are several ferries each day.

Slightly more expensive, but more direct from Europe, is to fly with Thai Airways direct to Phuket in Thailand; from here you cross the border to Kota Bharu.

Kuala Terengganu can be reached by road from Kuala Lumpur via Kuantan 455km (282 miles) and from Singapore via Johor Bahru and Kuantan 559km (347 miles). There are regular flights from Kuala Lumpur and from Singapore via Kuantan or Johor Bahru.

You should avoid August, which is the local holiday and high season. The resort closes down for the monsoon season, from the end of October until the beginning of March. May to July are particularly good times for diving.

Where to Stay

Medium Price Range
Coral View Island Resort, Pulau Perhentian Besar; tel 09-6956943/fax 010-9843943. Air conditioned and fan-cooled accommodation in idyllic surroundings.

Perhentian Island Resort, Pulau tel 09-6910946/fax 09-6977562; e-mail pir@po.jaring.my; www.jaring.my/perhentian/welcome.html. Kuala Lumpur Office: 22nd Floor Menara Promet, Jalan Sultan Promet, 50250 Kuala Lumpur. Postal Address: PO Box 10849, 50726 Kuala Lumpur; tel 03–2448530/fax 03–2434984. There are two standards of accommodation at Perhentian Island Resort. The cheaper 'A' frame chalets are built on a hill and have electric light and fans but no electrical sockets for charging.

More expensive are the bungalows, built on level ground near the restaurant. These have en suite toilets and showers, electric lights and fans, as well as three-square-pin electrical sockets (240 volts) for charging, etc.

Lower Price Range
The general standard is continually improving, with air-conditioned chalets as well as basic chalets. Accommodation that cannot easily be booked directly can be booked through:

Perhentian Ferry Travel & Tours Sdn. Bhd., 102-3, Jalan Besar, 22300 Kuala Besut, Terengganu; tel 09-6919679/mobile 019-9100367/fax 09-6919680; e-mail pferry@tm.net.my; www.perhentianferry.com.my

With some of the more basic accommodation you will need to carry your own food, bottled water and some form of lighting, with spare batteries or gas cartridges.

Coco Hut, Pulau Perhentian Besar; tel 010-9827546

Rosly's Chalets, Pulau Perhentian Kecil; tel

09-6910155

Where to Eat

There is little or nothing on offer by way of separate restaurants, so in general people use the restaurant attached to their accommodation.

Dive Facilities

There are now a number of diving operators on both Pulau Perhentian Besar and Pulau Perhentian Kecil, although the situation fluctuates. The operators mostly offer diving for fun or instruction up to advanced open water standard, though one is a full PADI 5-star IDC Centre.

Diver's World, Coral View Island Resort, Pulau Perhentian Besar; tel 09-6956943/fax 010-9843943

Flora Bay Divers, DS-42 Kompleks Letak Kereta Seksyen-9, 15000 Kota Bharu Kelantan; tel/fax 09-6977266. Also c/o Flora Bay Chalets and Resort, Pulau Perhentian Besar, 22300 Terengganu; tel/fax 09-6977266; e-mail fbdivers@hotmail.com

Perhentian Dive Centre, P.O. Box 27 - Kuala Besut, 22300 Terengganu; tel 012-9388083/fax 09-6910943; e-mail info@dive-malaysia.com; www.dive-malaysia.com. The first PADI 5-star IDC Centre on Pulau Perhentian.

Perhentian Island Resort
(See address above)
NAUI and PADI training.

Turtle Bay Divers, Longbeach (Pasir Panjang), Pulau Perhentian Kecil; tel 10-3336647, 09-3336647. Branch at Mama's Place Chalet, Pulau Perhentian Kecil; tel 10-3319624, 09-3319624 Main Office: Turtle Bay Divers, 3 Jalan 17/21F, 46400 Petaling Jaya; tel 03-7582527/fax 03-7560472; e-mail juarezp@tm.net.my; www.turtlebaydivers.com. PADI training.

Watercolours Dive Centre, c/o Paradise Resort, Pulau Perhentian Besar, Kuala Trengganu; tel 018-8931852; e-mail fredisoh@tm.net.my. PADI training to Divemaster level.

Dive Operators on Mainland East Coast
East Coast Dive Centre P.O. Box 25, Marang, 21600 Terengganu; tel 20-11971306

Eco Diving Sdn. Bhd. Eco Diving, 24, Tingkat Satu, Wisma Awang Chik, Jalan Sultan Mahmud, 20400 Kuala Terengganu; tel 09-6311262/fax 09-6236300
and
137A Jalan Sultan Zainal Abidin, 20000 Kuala Terengganu; tel 09-6311262/fax 09-6236300. PADI courses.

Endless Quests Beach Chalet Stingray Beach Chalet, Pantai Peranginan Merang, Setiu, 21010 Terengganu; tel 09-6531809. The two British World War II shipwrecks, the HMS *Prince of*

Wales and HMS *Repulse*, are now considered to be within the realms of technical divers.

Film Processing

No film processing is available on the island or in Kuala Besut. Kuala Terengganu has several mini-labs for processing print film.

Hospital

Terengganu General Hospital, Kuala Terengganu; tel 09–633333

Local Highlights

Pulau Perhentian Besar offers walks on its exquisite beaches and opportunities to go jungle trekking. If you want to go further afield in search of land-based experiences, your best option is the mainland, where you'll find coastal beach resorts, fishing villages and offshore islands. One highlight used to be watching the Leatherback Turtles coming ashore at Rantau Abang to lay their eggs, but sadly the number of Leatherbacks nesting here has collapsed, and what was once a spectacle is now barely worth a detour. Instead, you could take a trip to **Taman Negara National Park,** en route visiting **Lake Kenyir** – formed by the Kenyir Dam (finished 1985) – the **Sekayu waterfalls** and the **Batu Biwa caves.**

Kuala Terengganu, the major local population centre, is worth exploring: it has the **State Museum,** the **Maziah Palace,** the **Zainal Abidin Mosque** and various batik-printing, silk-weaving, songket-weaving and handicraft centres. You can see traditional-style boat-building on **Pulau Duyung Besar,** an island on the Terengganu River.

Northwards, across the state border into Kelantan, is **Kota Bharu,** with one of the largest and liveliest markets in Malaysia, as well as batik printing and local handicrafts; this is also the place to see kite-flying and top-spinning contests.

The further north you go towards the national border, the stronger becomes the Thai influence. **Wat Phothivihan,** at Tumpat, has one of the largest reclining Buddhas in Southeast Asia.

Depending on your schedule you may arrive in Kuala Terengganu or Kota Bharu too late to connect with the Perhentian ferry from Kuala Besut. If transfers prove a problem and you find you have to stay overnight, the following accommodation details may prove useful:

Upper Price Range
Primula Beach Resort, JL Persinggahan, PO Box 43, Kuala Terengganu; tel 09-6222100/fax 09-6233360; e-mail primula@po.jaring.my

Medium Price Range
Qurata Riverside Resort, Lot 175-19, Kuala IbaiKuala Terengganu; tel 09–675590/fax 09–675511

Lower Price Range
City Hotel, 97–99 Jl Banggol, Kuala Terengganu; tel 09-6221481

Pulau Redang
(Terengganu Marine Park)

There are nine islands in the Pulau Redang archipelago. The largest is Pulau Redang itself, followed by the much smaller Pulau Pinang and then seven tiny islets: Pulau Ekor Tebu, Pulau Kerengga Besar, Pulau Kerengga Kecil, Pulau Lima, Pulau Ling (often called Pulau Chipor), Pulau Paku Besar and Pulau Paku Kecil.

Situated 45km (28 miles) northeast of Kuala Terengganu and 27km (17 miles) off Merang, this area probably has the best coral reefs off Peninsular Malaysia, and certainly they are the most intensively studied.

I found the underwater visibility much better in Pulau Redang – about 30m (100ft) at all the sites – than off Pulau Perhentian (see page 48) and Pulau Tioman (see page 74).

Although rain is frequent throughout the year, the climate of the archipelago enjoys a wetter season during November to March, when the northeast monsoon is blowing.

KAMPUNG KUALA REDANG

The fishing village of Kampung Kuala Redang, built on stilts at the estuary of the Sungai Redang on Pulau Redang, is home to about 200 families who moved here from Pulau Pinang, just opposite, several years ago. The people subsist mainly on fishing, though some supplement their income by collecting edible swiftlets' nests (from the caves along the northeast coast) as well as turtles' eggs, 50% of which are – or are supposed to be – sold to

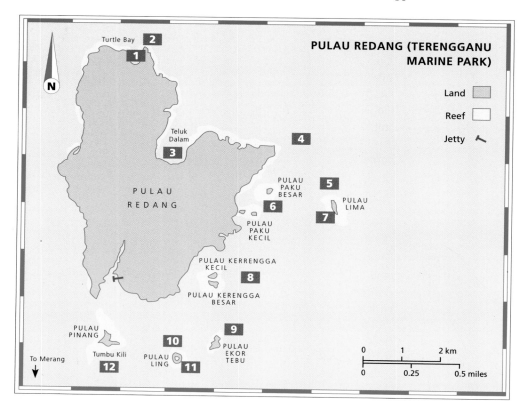

the hatchery managed by the Department of Fisheries. There is some agriculture on the flat land of the Sungai Redang Valley, including fruit trees on the hillsides. You can still see remnants of the old coconut and pepper plantations.

REEF-LIFE

The beaches are sandy on the east side of Pulau Redang and stony on the island's west side. The waters separating Pulau Redang from the small islets are relatively shallow (up to 25m; 82ft). The most extensive reefs are around these islets, showing the greatest variety on the deeper north and east sides. There are shallow reef flats and coral gardens dominated by staghorn, table and boulder corals. In places where the cliffs are steep you can find soft corals, encrusting corals and sea anemones on the granite. All told, 52 genera of hard corals are reported in these waters, plus 43 genera of crustaceans, 57 species of marine algae, 36 species of marine worms and 82 species of molluscs. Hawksbill and Green Turtles nest along the west coast of Pulau Redang, and while I was diving there I saw a Leatherback Turtle. Reef fish and pelagic species are plentiful, and Manta Rays and Whale Sharks are often seen in the open waters around Pulau Redang.

FAUNA

The islands' fauna is impoverished by comparison with that of the mainland – the inland forest bird fauna, for example, includes only nine species (plus migrants). Scant as it is, the fauna has evolved in the absence of carnivorous predators, and is therefore vulnerable to introduced species, so it is worrying that the new resort has plans to establish an aviary, a butterfly farm, flower and orchid farms and a crocodile farm.

ACCOMMODATION

There is now good accommodation available on Pulau Redang, as well as more simple accommodation. The more basic resorts make little effort to keep their lovely beaches clean of drift rubbish and not much to dispose of garbage: monkeys, squirrels and insects attracted by this rubbish can be a nuisance – I soon learned to shut all my equipment away when I was out after we found a squirrel eating the silicone rubber of my buddy's facemask.

The Department of Fisheries Visitor Centre on Pulau Pinang, where there are also Marine Park's Staff Quarters and a research station, is beautifully clean and has delightful

---

MALAYSIA'S FIRST MARINE PARK

The marine waters surrounding the Pulau Redang archipelago to a distance of 5.6km (3 nautical miles) from the low-water marks of the shores of the islands were in 1985 designated a Marine Park — Malaysia's first. (Before that, from 1983, they were Prohibited Fisheries waters.) The Marine Park is administered by the Department of Fisheries. Most dive sites have fixed mooring buoys to stop anchor damage.

Core Zone
No fishing or shell collecting is allowed within the core zone, defined as 1 nautical mile (1.85km) from the islands' low-water marks; in the outer zone, between this limit and the 3-nautical-mile boundary, trawl-fishing, fish-traps and spear-fishing are forbidden, although resident fishermen are permitted to practise traditional non-destructive fishing and visitors can indulge in rod-and-line fishing with the requisite permit from the Department of Fisheries.

The news is not entirely good, however. Before protection was enforced by the Prohibited Fisheries status, shell life was overcollected and blast-fishing, trawling and spear-fishing were common, and it will be a while before the area recovers. Also, immediately outside the Park's boundary, night-time line and squid-fishing with lights are permitted. This almost certainly has the effect of deterring many of the turtles who would otherwise come here to nest, and also attracts some fish species out of the protected area to places where they can be legally caught. Moreover, while the designated waters might be protected, the Marine Park legislation does not extend to cover activities on the islands. This goes in the teeth of the prevailing wisdom about Marine Parks, which has it that, if they are to be at all effective, activities on the adjoining land areas must also be controlled.

flower gardens, turtle hatchlings, maps, information brochures and exhibits. It is well worth a visit in its own right.

SNORKELLING

You can snorkel off the turtle-nesting beaches of Pasir Mak Kapit and Pasir Mak Simpan and off the west coast of Pulau Redang, but the turtles are almost the sole interest here as the fish life is not good. The main diving and snorkelling areas are off the east coast and, in particular, off the small islets. The southwest coast of Pulau Pinang generally offers good diving in shallow water, to 18m (60ft). The northeast coast of Pulau Pinang is good for snorkelling.

1 TURTLE BAY
2 TANJUNG BATU TOKONG

★★★

Location: The northernmost coast of Pulau Redang and Turtle Bay.
Access: By boat.
Conditions: Sheltered in Turtle Bay; off Tanjung Batu Tokong it can be rough, with strong currents.
In calm weather you can snorkel all along the north and northeast coasts, with turtles on view in all the bays. At Turtle Bay as many as 22 turtles have been seen at one time. At Tanjung Batu Tokong the jumbles of large boulders bear soft corals and gorgonian sea fans, and there is good fish life here as well.

3 TELUK DALAM

★★★

Location: The large bay of Teluk Dalam.
Access: Either off the beaches in the bay or by boat from elsewhere.
Conditions: Sheltered outside the monsoon season.
Another bay where you can find turtles. The fish life is good, especially at the base of the rocks, which form caves and overhangs. There is a coral garden with a wide variety of hard and soft corals, including encrusting corals, table corals, mushroom and boulder corals.

4 TANJUNG GUA KAWAH

★★★

Location: The easternmost point of Pulau Redang, north of Pulau Paku Besar.
Access: By boat.
Conditions: This area tends to have strong surface and deep-water currents, so experienced divers should check the conditions before their less experienced companions enter the water.
Average depth: 15m (50ft)
Maximum depth: 20m (65ft)
A jumble of rocks descends to sand. The strong deep-water currents keep coral growth down, but as partial compensation there is abundant fish life, especially sheltering in the caves and under overhangs among the rocks. You might also see some pelagic species.

5 BIG SEAMOUNT

★★★★★

Location: Approximately 50m (165ft) north of Pulau Lima, east of Pulau Paku Besar.
Access: By boat to the buoy over the seamount.
Conditions: Normally calm; can become choppy and have a strong current after bad weather.
Average depth: 25m (82ft)
Maximum depth: Beyond 40m (130ft)
The diving all around Pulau Lima is excellent, and this oval seamount in particular is considered by many to offer Peninsular Malaysia's most spectacular diving. It is a jumble of boulders with its longer axis oriented east–west; it rises from a depth of 30m (100ft), on the landward side, to within 10m (33ft) of the surface. The flat top is covered in hard corals, leathery soft corals,

encrusting corals, mushroom corals, tunicates and sponges, gorgonian sea fans and sea anemones with attendant clownfish.

The seaward slope, which continues down to a depth of more than 40m (130ft), has a variety of whip corals and in the deeper waters, dark green *Tubastrea micranthus* branch-like cup corals, large *Dendronephthya* soft tree corals and nudibranchs.

The fish life found here includes all the expected angelfish, butterflyfish and wrasse; there are also many species of parrotfish, pufferfish and triggerfish, plus damselfish, sergeant majors, scorpionfish, lionfish (including Zebra Lionfish), stonefish, moray eels, Blue-spotted Ribbontail Rays, soldierfish, squirrelfish, batfish, groupers and barracuda. In the open water there are shoals of fusiliers, jacks and snappers, at least two varieties of jellyfish and the occasional turtle. Cardinalfish and sweepers congregate in the caves.

There are fan worms on the sand and Christmas Tree Worms in the boulder corals, and also on view are several varieties of sea cucumbers, sea stars, cushion stars and sea urchins.

6 PULAU PAKU BESAR: SOUTH SIDE

★★★★

Location: Pulau Paku Besar lies, 1/2km (1/3 mile) east of Pulau Redang.
Access: By boat.
Conditions: Normally calm, but can become choppy and have a strong current after bad weather. Snorkelling is possible in the shallow water near the cliffs.
Average depth: 15m (50ft)
Maximum depth: 21m (70ft)
Cliffs slope down at an angle of 30–40° to a level bottom where there are lots of whip, staghorn, table, lettuce and mushroom corals; the cliffs themselves are covered in leathery soft corals, small *Dendronephthya* soft corals and many feather stars. Also on view are some big Giant Clams plus several other species of shellfish and tunicates. The fish life, though not prolific, includes many species of wrasse, pufferfish and triggerfish, as well as all the expected angelfish and butterflyfish, damselfish, sergeant majors and batfish.

In the deeper water there are small gorgonian sea fans, large *Dendronephthya* soft tree corals, some dark green *Tubastrea micranthus* cup corals and several species of nudibranchs, while in the open water you have a chance of seeing at least two species of jellyfish and shoals of jacks, fusiliers and snappers. On the bottom live many varieties of sea cucumbers, sea stars and sea urchins, but very few sea anemones.

7 PULAU LIMA: WEST SIDE AND SOUTH END

★★★★★

Location: Pulau Lima lies 2km (1¼ miles) east of Pulau Paku Kecil.
Access: By boat.
Conditions: Normally calm; can become choppy and have a strong current after bad weather.
Average depth: 24m (80ft)
Maximum depth: 30m (100ft)
I dived here immediately after my arrival from Pulau Tioman (see page 74), and the clear visibility (about 30m/100ft) did wonders in raising my spirits! All of the diving around Pulau Lima is pretty spectacular. Here off Pulau Lima you find the usual jumble of boulders dropping steeply to 20m (65ft), then gently down to sand at 30m (100ft). There is the same wide variety of corals, sponges and fish life as at Big Seamount (Site 5). The west side has rather more sea anemones with clownfish and also more boulder corals with Christmas Tree Worms, plus lots of good staghorn, table, mushroom and lettuce corals. The boulders at the island's southern end offer further caves and tunnels in which you can spot cardinalfish, sweepers and invertebrates hiding.

8 MINI SEAMOUNT

★★★★★

Location: 100m (330ft) east of Pulau Kerengga Besar.
Access: By boat to the buoy over the seamount.
Conditions: Usually calm and more sheltered than Pulau Lima, but can get rough with a current after bad weather. The usual clear visibility found off these islands.
Average depth: 18m (60ft)
Maximum depth: 20m (65ft)
A small seamount consisting of a jumble of boulders down to sand at 20m (65ft). The deeper rocks are covered in leathery soft corals, with some *Dendronephthya* soft tree corals and dark green *Tubastrea micranthus* cup corals, tunicates and encrusting corals and sponges. There are sea anemones everywhere.

The abundant marine life is similar to that at Pulau Lima (Site 7), but with more varieties of pufferfish and groupers, more turtles and fewer stony corals. On the landward side you should be able to see several species of immature fish.

On the sand there are big *Dendronephthya* soft tree corals and many large barrel sponges covered with Alabaster Sea Cucumbers.

The channel, 15m (50ft) deep, between Pulau Kerengga Kecil and Pulau Kerengga Besar is good for snorkelling. There is a colourful coral garden with staghorn, lettuce and mushroom corals. Off the south-west side of Pulau Kerengga Besar is a large area of mushroom corals.

9 PULAU EKOR TEBU: NORTHEAST CORNER

★★★★★

Location: Pulau Ekor Tebu lies 2¹/₂ km (1¹/₂ miles) east of Pulau Pinang and northeast of Pulau Ling.
Access: By boat.
Conditions: Normally calm; can be choppy with a strong current after bad weather.
Average depth: 19m (62ft)
Maximum depth: 24m (80ft)
The northeast corner is the deepest part of the waters off Pulau Ekor Tebu: boulders extend northwards, dropping steeply to 10m (33ft) and then at a more gentle gradient to 24m (80ft).

There is an underwater cave at 20m (65ft), and some 30m out from the cave is a rock outcrop which may break the surface at low tide.

I dived this site as a drift-dive after a heavy storm. Despite the rough night the visibility was excellent. There were fish and jellyfish everywhere, but what attracted me most were the table and lettuce corals, which were of the quality more commonly associated with Pulau Sipadan (see page 130) and Pulau Sangalaki (see page 143), off Borneo, and the Tubbataha Reefs in the Philippines Sulu Sea.

There are also healthy staghorn corals, many large Giant Clams and several shells. The fish life is generally similar to if not so concentrated as that at Pulau Lima (Site 7), but I did also see here a cuttlefish, squid and an Eagle Ray.

10 BATU CHIPOR

★★★★

Location: Marked by a buoy 20m (70ft) from a tiny rock pinnacle just breaking the surface north of Pulau Ling (Pulau Chipor), east of Pulau Ekor Tebu.
Access: By boat to the buoy.
Conditions: Usually calm; can be choppy with a current after bad weather.
Average depth: 8m (26ft)
Maximum depth: 15m (50ft)
A pretty wall, covered in small colourful *Dendronephthya* soft tree corals, leathery corals and gorgonian sea fans, goes down to a flat sandy bottom where there are lots of staghorn, table, mushroom and lettuce corals and some boulder corals with Christmas Tree Worms.

Interestingly, there are not so many fish as there are

at the other dives in the Pulau Redang group, but most of the local angelfish and butterflyfish, pufferfish, lionfish, parrotfish, wrasses, groupers, cuttlefish and Blue-spotted Lagoon Rays are present.

At sand level there are moray eels, nudibranchs as well as a variety of species of sea cucumbers, sea stars and cushion stars.

11 PULAU LING

★★★

Location: The small islet of Pulau Ling, east of Pulau Pinang, southwest of Pulau Ekor Tebu.
Access: By boat.
Conditions: Well sheltered and therefore usually calm although bad weather from the south can adversely affect this area, but otherwise only the foulest weather will cause you any problems.
Average depth: 10m (33ft)
Maximum depth: 20m (65ft)
The main attractions of this islet are two enormous boulder corals (*Porites* species), the bigger of which is 40m (130ft) in circumference and 10m (33ft) in height, with a cave 2m (6ft) high at its base. These boulder corals are the largest known coral structures off the east coast of Peninsular Malaysia, and are estimated to be many hundreds of years old.

Also of interest in the area are the marvellous staghorn, table and lettuce corals, mushroom corals, soft corals, sponges, tunicates, sea anemones and gorgonian sea fans.

12 TUMBU KILI

★★★★★

Location: This small rock breaks the surface just off Tanjung Tumbu Kili, the southernmost point of Pulau Pinang.
Access: By boat.
Conditions: Well sheltered and therefore usually calm; bad weather from the south can adversely affect this area, but otherwise only the foulest weather will make diving difficult.
Average depth: 10m (33ft)
Maximum depth: 20m (65ft)
Below the low-tide mark, down to sand at 20m (65ft), the jumble of boulders here is carpeted with leathery and *Dendronephthya* soft corals, gorgonian sea fans and sea anemones. On the sand itself are larger *Dendronephthya* soft corals and gorgonian sea fans, whip corals, some staghorn corals, table corals, mushroom corals and boulder corals, nudibranchs, sea cucumbers, sea stars, cushion stars, Giant Clams and shells. Hundreds of long-

tentacled jellyfish and many shoals of fish – including parrotfish, jacks, trevallies, snappers, fusiliers, soldierfish, sweepers and wrasse – swim out in the open water. You can also see several species of pufferfish, angelfish and butterflyfish, some barracuda, batfish and Bumphead Parrotfish. There are feather stars on all the whip corals and gorgonian sea fans. Further out on the sand barrel sponges are common.

GORGONIANS

Gorgonians, like their relatives the stony corals, are colonial animals made up of numerous anemone-like polyps sharing a common, flexible skeleton of keratin, which is similar to the material in animal horn. There are literally hundreds of different species of gorgonians and they occur in a variety of forms including whips, harps, fans and bushes that may grow to as large as 3 or 4 metres. A mature colony of gorgonians may take many years to grow but can be spectacular. They grow in abundance in tropical waters, in a variety of stunning colours and are perhaps most interesting to observe at night when the polyps are feeding.

Pulau Redang (Terengganu Marine Park)

HOW TO GET THERE

You can reach Pulau Redang by boat from either Kuala Terengganu or Merang. The shortest boat trip is from sleepy Merang (not to be confused with Marang), 38km (24 miles) north of Kuala Terengganu; a fast speedboat from here takes just over 1hr. You can get to Merang (or to Kuala Besut) from Kuala Terengganu by bus or taxi. Kuala Terengganu can be reached by road from Kuala Lumpur via Kuantan, 455km (282 miles), and from Singapore via Johor Bahru and Kuantan 559km (347 miles). There are regular flights from Kuala Lumpur and from Singapore via Kuantan or Johor Bahru.

WHERE TO STAY

Upper Price Range
Berjaya Redang Golf & Country Resort and **Berjaya Redang Beach Resort,** P.O. Box 126, Pejabat Pos Besar, 20928 Kuala Terengganu; tel 09-6971111/fax 09-6971100; e-mail red@hr.berjaya.com.my; www.berjayaresorts.com.my/redangbeach/index.html. Part of the Best Western Berjaya Group.

Coral Redang Island Resort, 24, 1st Floor, Wisma Awang Chik, Jalan Sultan Mahmud, 20400 Kuala Terengganu; tel 09-6236200/fax 09-6236300. Quality accommodation.

Redang Bay Resort, 139, Jalan Bandar, 21210 Kuala Terengganu; tel 09-6236048/fax 09-6242048; e-mail redangbay@malaysia.crosswinds.net; www.redangbay.com.my. Quality accommodation aimed at local trade, with disco and restaurant serving local cuisine.

Redang Beach Resort, 1st Floor, 147, Jalan Bandar, 21210 Kuala Terengganu; tel 09-6238188

Redang Pelangi Resort, 27, Jalan Bandar, 21210 Kuala Terengganu; tel 09-6223158/fax 09-6235202. Quality accommodation.

DIVE FACILITIES

The problems that I experienced on my first visit, when there was very little diving equipment on the islands, are now long gone. The new quality resorts provide all that divers need and there are regular ferries.

Since 1999, the authorities have levied a small fee on visitors to help fund protecting the natural environment, cleaning the beaches, maintaining the dive site marker buoys, eradicating Crown-of-Thorns Starfish and the 'Save the Turtles' project (SEATRU).

Berjaya Redang Golf & Country Resort and **Berjaya Redang Beach Resort,** P.O. Box 126, Pejabat Pos Besar, 20928 Kuala Terengganu; tel 09-6971111/fax 09-6971100; e-mail red@hr.berjaya.com.my. PADI training.

Leisure Divers Sdn. Bhd., (at Redang Reefs Resort), Lot No 25-UG-13 Plaza Prima, Old Klang Road 58200, Kuala Lumpur; tel/fax 03-7826059; e-mail jeffdive@tm.net.my; http://members.xoom.com/leisurediver. SSI Open Water & Advanced courses.

Redang Bay Resort, 139, Jalan Bandar, 21210 Kuala Terengganu; tel 09-6236048/fax 09-6242048; e-mail redangbay@malaysia.crosswinds.net; www.redangbay.com.my. NAUI and PADI training to open water.

Scuba Quest Sdn. Bhd., c/o Coral Redang Island Resort, Pualau Redang; tel/fax 09-6531180; e-mail info@scuba-quest.com.my; www.scuba-quest.com.my Kuala Lumpur Office: Lot 3-38, 2nd Floor, Wisma Central, Jalan Ampany, 50450 Kuala Lumpur; tel 011-973705/fax 09-6696270 Kuala Terengganu Office: CA 104 Taman Sri Kolam, 20000 Kuala Terengganu; tel 09-6311262. NAUI and PADI training to Divemaster.

FILM PROCESSING

None available on the islands. Kuala Terengganu has several mini-labs for processing print film, but for E6 processing you have to go to Johor Bahru or Kuala Lumpur.

HOSPITAL

Terengganu General Hospital, Kuala Terengganu; tel 09–633333

LOCAL HIGHLIGHTS

The islands' flora and fauna are quite interesting. For details of local highlights on the mainland opposite, refer to the directory covering Pulau Perhentian (page 57).

The Crown-of-Thorns Starfish, *Acanthaster planci*, first gained notoriety in the 1960s and 1970s, when it was observed that hugely increasing populations were causing massive coral-reef destruction in the Indo-Pacific, particularly on Australia's Great Barrier Reef and the reefs of Southern Japan, and later off the islands of Micronesia (especially Guam) and to a lesser extent in the Red Sea.

ENVIRONMENTAL CONCERN

These early observations caused panic among scientists and environmentalists. Some blamed the depletion of the creature's natural predators, such as the Triton Shell, pufferfish, triggerfish and Humphead Wrasse; others pointed out that many of the worst-hit areas had been affected by blast fishing, harbour construction, dredging and pollution, with consequent decline of the smaller creatures and some corals that eat *Acanthaster planci* at the egg and larval stage (a female Crown-of-Thorns Starfish can produce 12–24 million eggs annually).

However, analysis of core samples drilled through the Great Barrier Reef suggests such population explosions have occurred regularly throughout history, and it may be just that, as scuba diving has become ever more popular, there are many more divers and marine scientists in the water to observe the changes.

DEVASTATION

The stark white skeletons of *Acropora* corals killed by aggregations of *Acanthaster planci* are a terrible sight: in some cases 80–90% coral destruction occurs. Many attempts have been made to eradicate the starfish during local population explosions, but none has been fully effective.

A FEARSOME CREATURE

About 30cm (12in) across, with up to 23 arms covered on the dorsal surface with short fat spines – 3–5cm (0.8–2in) long – *Acanthaster planci* varies in colour from orange to green/blue and purple. The spines contain a nasty venom that gives some people a severe reaction, ranging from a skin rash to nausea and severe pain. Unlike many other predators on coral, *Acanthaster planci* does not damage the coral skeleton: only live coral tissues are eaten. It feeds on the polyps, preferably those of *Acropora* table corals, by everting its stomach over the coral so that the digestive enzymes come into direct contact with the coral tissue; thus digestion starts before the food is taken into the mouth. These enzymes may be the cause of the severe skin reaction suffered by divers who are foolish enough to pick the creatures up without gloves.

The Crown-of-Thorns Starfish regularly returns to the same coral table until that table is dead. When aggregations of these creatures occur, newcomers are attracted to the coral table. It is likely that attractant chemicals are given off during feeding.

Normally *Acanthaster planci* feeds at night, preferring to hide deep in crevices during the day. When aggregations occur, many of the individuals involved make less effort to hide during the day, often only crawling into the shade of the coral table's underside. Others can be seen before dusk moving through shady areas towards their prey.

EFFECTIVE EXTERMINATION

Damaged Crown-of-Thorns Starfish soon regenerate. Injections with formaldehyde, copper sulphate or sodium hypochlorite are expensive, slow and inefficient. The only successful way of exterminating the creatures is to bring them ashore en masse and bury them – or, better still, burn them. This was how the Malaysian Fisheries Department (with private-sector backing) combated the recent major infestation at Pulau Redang. The good news is that on a recent visit to Pulau Redang I saw few Crown-of-Thorns Starfish, and those reefs unaffected by the resort construction were regenerating well.

Crown-of-Thorns Starfish (Acanthaster planci). These voracious predators sometimes occur in large aggregations, completely decimating large areas of live stony corals.

and jacks, all the expected angelfish and butterflyfish, wrasse, bream, batfish, hawkfish, surgeonfish, triggerfish and pufferfish. Whale Sharks, Manta Rays and Eagle Rays are sometimes seen. On the sand are moray eels, lizardfish, lionfish, scorpionfish, stonefish, Blue-spotted Lagoon Rays, stingrays, crocodilefish, sea cucumbers, sea stars (including Crown-of-Thorns Starfish), cushion stars, sea urchins and fan worms.

5 6 THE TWO BAYS ON THE EAST SIDE OF PULAU TENGGOL

★★★★

Location: On the east side of Pulau Tenggol, south of the lighthouse, between the lighthouse and Tanjung Pisang and between Tanjung Pisang and Tanjung Sarang Lang.
Access: By boat.
Conditions: You would snorkel here only in calm weather; there can be some strong currents. Visibility can reach 20m (65ft).
Average depth: 5m (16ft)
Maximum depth: Whatever you can snorkel
Both bays have sandy bottoms with rocks and coral heads harbouring sponges, sea anemones with and without clownfish, stingrays, lionfish, scorpionfish, angelfish, butterflyfish, triggerfish, pufferfish, parrotfish, surgeonfish, hawkfish, bream and fan worms.

On the sand itself are lizard fish, gobies, seastars, sea cucumbers and sea urchins. If you are lucky you may spot a turtle.

7 TELUK AIR TAWAR

★★★★★★★★

Location: The house-reef off the resorts in Teluk Air Tawar.
Access: Off the beach in front of the resorts.
Conditions: Well sheltered, except from very bad weather. The visibility, at 20m (65ft), is low for this region.
Average depth: 12m (40ft)
Maximum depth: 34m (110ft)
The house-reef slopes off to sand, where there is a colony of garden eels, at 25m (82ft), plus the usual boulder outcrops as well as fan worms. The boulders are well covered with sponges and corals, both stony and soft as well as encrusting. In deeper water are larger *Dendronephthya* soft corals as well as all the fish life generally found in the area, but in concentrations less than those prevalent off the headland to the south.

8 DRIFTING FROM BATU CHANCHANG TO TANJUNG GEMOK

★★★★★

Location: The southwest side of the reef from Batu Chanchang through Tanjung Pasir Tingara to Tanjung Gemok.
Access: By boat (10–15min) anticlockwise around Tanjung Gemok from Teluk Air Tawar.
Conditions: Usually calm, with a current along the coast that can be strong; novices should be accompanied by a divemaster.
Average depth: 24m (80ft)
Maximum depth: 34m (110ft)
Considered by many the best dive in the area, this is, like Site 3, often referred to as the 'highway' because of the concentration of fish life seen here. The bottom is a collection of rock outcrops on sand, with good coral cover – both stony and soft as well as plenty of encrusting corals, sea anemones, sponges and nudibranchs. However, it is the fish fauna that is the main attraction. There are shoals of jacks, trevallies, snappers, fusiliers, barracuda, tuna and Bumphead Parrotfish. Then there are all the local angelfish and butterflyfish, plus surgeonfish, triggerfish, unicornfish, parrotfish, Eagle Rays, bream, hawkfish, batfish, wrasse and pufferfish. On the sand are lionfish, stonefish, scorpionfish, crocodilefish, moray eels, Blue-spotted Ribbontail Rays, stingrays and lizardfish, while on every high point there are feather stars spreading themselves out in the current.

Previous page: *Feather star (Comanthus bennetti). When at rest during the daytime feather stars tuck their arms inwards.*

Adventure, are highly organized and are costed for the international market. The many smaller dive operators on the island cost less; however, they are mainly oriented towards giving introductory courses to visiting tourists, and so serious divers may find them rather laid-back. The details of these smaller operators are always in flux as the cheaper resorts that they work from are bought out by developers for upgrading.

All the operators have dive-shops and offer dive equipment for rent.

Dive Asia Dive Shop, Tanjung Salang, Pulau Tioman, Pahang; tel 09-4195017/fax 09-4195010)
Postal Address:
Duncan Dominic, 169 Jalan Bukit, 86800 Mersing, Johor; tel 07–794098 (office), 07–793014 (residence)/fax 07–794099. PADI IDC Centre and Nitrox fills. Courses from Introduction up to Assistant Instructor.

DiveAsia Tioman Island, 27-A, Jalan Abu Bakar, 86800 Mersing; tel 07-7994098; fax 07-7994099; e-mail diveasia@tm.my. PADI and TDI Nitrox training.

Bali Hai Divers, Panuba Inn resort fax 06-3343271. PADI training and facilities for underwater photography.

B.J. Diving Centre, Kampung Air Batang; tel 09-4195555/fax 09-4195554; e-mail bjtioman@tm.net.my; www.e-my.net.my/pahang/bjdivetioman/tioman.html
and
380 Jalan Bakawali, Taman Sri Mersing, 86800 Mersing. PADI 5-star IDC and IANTD facility, Nitrox and Trimix.

Divers US (Jasper Bell), Kampung Tekek, Pulau Tioman, 86807 Pahang; tel 011–352776 (mobile)/fax 03–8375897. PADI courses.

Ianz Dive Shop, Mokhtar's Place, Teluk Air Batang, 86800 Pulau Tioman; tel 07-376401/fax 07-324210). PADI courses.

Octo Diving Den, Mastura Resort, Kampung Tekek; tel 03-2417905/fax 03-2418004. PADI, SSI and IANTD courses.

Scuba Point, Kampung Tekek, 86807 Tioman; tel/fax 09-4191228; e-mail tiomanmalaysia@hotmail.com

Tioman Dive Centre & Mukut Village Resort, 1, Jalan Sultanah, 86000 Kluang, Johor; tel 07-7737711

Tioman Reef Divers (Reeno C.L. Chew), c/o Babura Chalet, Kampung Tekek, Pulau Tioman, 86800 Pahang; tel 011-767502. NAUI and PADI training.

Berjaya Tioman Beach Resort
Kampung Tekek; tel 09-4191000/fax 09-4191718; e-mail tod@hr.berjaya.com.my; www.berjayaresorts.com.my/tioman/index.html
Head Office:
Berjaya Hotels and Resorts, Level 19, Shazan Prudential Tower, 30, Jalan Sultan Ismail, 50250 Kuala Lumpur; tel 03-2429611/fax 03-2442527; e-mail bhr@hr.berjaya.com.my; www.berjayaresorts.com.my
Singapore Office:
Berjaya Hotels and Resorts Singapore Ltd., 67, Tanjung Pagar Road, Singapore 088488; tel 2273688/fax 2254966; e-mail berjaya@singnet.com.sg. PADI training to Assistant Instructor. I met divers who preferred the Berjaya Tioman Beach Resort because of its superior accommodation and the fact that it has its own jetty for ferries and offers transport by road to the airport, but who booked their actual diving with the cheaper operators.

Film Processing

None is available on the island or in Mersing; the nearest is in Johor Bahru or Kuala Lumpur.

Hospitals

There is a very small hospital on the island (tel 09–445347) and a similar one in Mersing (tel 07–793333). In addition there is the main hospital in Johor Bahru:

Hospital Sultanah Aminah
tel 07–231666

However, with the STOL-aircraft service, it is just as easy to fly to Kuala Lumpur or Singapore.

Local Highlights

Pulau Tioman is an island to relax on; most visitors go there only for the beaches and coral reefs. There are small secluded beaches all round the island. **Berjaya Tioman Beach Resort** has a first-class golf course, and offers also horse-riding and all watersports. You can walk along most of the west coast, although the path gets faint in places. The forest is full of interesting wildlife, and the trees keep the path pleasantly shady. One popular walk traverses the

island from **Kampung Tekek** (Lizard Village) to **Kampung Juara** (Catfish Village), starting beside the mosque in Kampung Tekek. The path climbs steeply through the forest, following the River Besar to its highest point; about halfway, there is a small waterfall off to the right. The slopes are more gradual on the Juara side. The whole walk takes about 3hr, and if you're tired at the end of it you can take the waterbus back.

Apart from the short climb over the headland just south of Nazri's Place, there is also a good walking path from Air Batang Bay to Kampung Tekek; this takes 30min, and you can then carry on for a further 30min along the road to reach the Berjaya Tioman Beach Resort. A poor path, faint in places, leads from here to Kampung Genting. A similar path runs from Air Batang Bay to Kampung Salang – about a 2hr walk.

The waterbus is worth at least a ride or two. As well as travelling between Kampung Salang, Kampung Air Batang, Kampung Tekek and the Berjaya Tioman Beach Resort, it runs two trips daily round the island, including stops at **Kampung Juara** and **Kampung Asah**, from where it is approximately 10min walk to the waterfall.

Over on the mainland is the little town of Kota Tinggi, 42km (26 miles) from Johor Bahru on the road between Mersing and Johor Bahru. Some 15km (9 miles) northwest of Kota Tinggi, on Gunung Muntahak, the Lumbong waterfalls are recommended, although they tend to be crowded at weekends. The **Endau Rompin National Park** has undisturbed rainforest and Orang Asli villages. Quite a lot further afield are the **Cameron Highlands** and **Taman Negara National Park**.

Encounters with turtles are a highlight of diving and snorkelling. There are some areas off Malaysia and Singapore where such encounters can be virtually guaranteed. Green and Hawksbill Turtles are found in large numbers off the northeastern coast of Sabah and across to the reefs of Tubbataha, in the Sulu Sea. Divers will find that Pulau Sipadan is the 'Turtle Capital of the World'.

ENDANGERED SPECIES
Of the seven oceanic turtle species – all of which are on the endangered-species list – six can be found in Malaysian waters: the Green Turtle (*Chelonia mydas*), the Hawksbill Turtle (*Eretmochelys imbricata*), the Loggerhead Turtle (*Caretta caretta*), the Leatherback Turtle (*Dermochelys coriacea*), the Pacific Olive Ridley Turtle (*Lepidochelys olivacea*) and the Flatback Turtle (*Natator depressus*). Four of these – the Green, Hawksbill, Leatherback and Pacific Olive Ridley – regularly nest on Malaysian beaches.

The two most commonly encountered are the Green and the Hawksbill. They may be difficult to distinguish underwater, where both appear a mottled dull green. However, the Green Turtle is usually larger,and has only one pair of prefrontal scales. The Hawksbill has a distinct beak; the outer edge of the latter's shell is usually jagged.

TURTLE FACTS

- Both on land and at sea, turtles often appear to be shedding tears. On land, the 'tears' are believed to prevent the eyes from becoming dehydrated and to cleanse them of sand. They possibly also help get rid of salt.

- As turtles are often observed copulating for as long as two hours, local people believe their meat and eggs have aphrodisiac properties. This hypothesis is unsupported by science.

- The bodies of marine turtles are entirely covered by a firm shell, only the head, limbs and tail protruding. Unlike their land counterparts, marine turtles cannot retract their head and limbs, so these are vulnerable to sharks and other predators. However, turtles can survive with missing limbs, and often do.

- The way that turtles swim is analogous to the flight of birds, the flippers moving up and down rather than to and fro.

THE GREEN TURTLE
The Green Turtle can reach a length of 1.2m (4ft) and weigh 135–180kg (3–400 pounds). The male is usually smaller than the female, but has a longer tail. The Green Turtle is mainly nocturnal and herbivorous, feeding on sea grasses, in daytime sleeping on the bottom, under coral heads or in caves. It nests on remote islands and lays eggs in the sand at the top of the beach, where they will be shaded by overhanging vegetation. The Loggerhead Turtle is similar to the Green but has a larger head. It feeds on fish, molluscs and crustacea.

THE HAWKSBILL TURTLE
The Hawksbill Turtle is the smallest turtle species, reaching a maximum length of 85cm (33in). In young individuals the plates of the carapace overlap; in adults they merely adjoin, and have characteristic brown and yellow markings of tortoiseshell. Hawksbills are usually carnivores, feeding on fish, molluscs, sponges and crustacea, although I have seen them eating algae. They nest by day or by night, preferring beaches along sheltered bays.

THE LEATHER BACK TURTLE
The relatively thin, heart-shaped carapace of the Leatherback Turtle has the appearance of brown leather and bears seven longitudinal ridges. It is the largest marine turtle, reaching nearly 2m (6^1/2ft) in length and weighing up to about 450kg (1000 pounds). The greatly reduced weight of the carapace, the more streamlined shape and the long flippers enable the Leatherback to swim at up to 10kph (6mph) and to cover huge distances – up to 5900km (3650 miles), according to the records – as it migrates after its prey, jellyfish, which are at the mercy of ocean currents.

Opposite top: *Female Green Turtle, Chelonia mydas.*
Opposite centre: *Young Hawksbill Turtle, Eretmochelys imbricata, showing the overlapping plates of the carapace.*
Opposite bottom: *The extremely rare Pacific Olive Ridley Turtle (Lepidochelys olivacea).*

HOW TO GET THERE

There are 'express' buses to Mersing from Johor Bahru, 135km (85 miles) to the south, and from Kuantan, 190km (120 miles) to the north. Long-distance buses from Singapore also stop here (see the directory covering Pahang Marine Parks, page 80). From where the bus drops you off it is an easy walk (10–15min) to the jetty. If you've come by car, you can leave the vehicle in the jetty's car park. Around the jetty you'll find offices representing each of the islands. It's a good idea to buy not only your boat ticket but also your accommodation here – or at one of the travel agencies in Mersing – rather than wait until you get to your destination island, since otherwise you are quite likely to find yourself with nowhere to stay. Travel times to the islands vary from about 1½hr to 4hr. If you need to change money, do so in Mersing – there is a licensed money changer in Jalan Abu Bakar, just opposite Golden Mal Tours – because the exchange rates you will be offered on the islands are exorbitant.

Since the 'express' buses stop at Mersing only en route to Johor Bahru, Kuantan or Singapore, it can be difficult during holiday periods to get a seat on one when you want to leave Mersing at the end of your stay, so it is a good idea to try to book in advance. Failing that, taxis to Johor Bahru or Kuantan are not prohibitively expensive – about 50% more than the bus fare.

Pulau Sibu is one of the larger and more popular islands. Boats go to it from Mersing or Tanjung Leman but, since it is further south, it can easily be reached by visitors from Singapore using ferries from Tanjong Sedili Besar at Teluk Mahkota (Jason's Bay).

WHERE TO STAY

Pulau Babi Besar
Radin Island Resort 1880 Jalan Jamaluang, Taman Mersing, 86800 Mersing; tel 07-7994152/fax 07-7991413

Besar Marina Resort c/o #10 Tourist Information Centre, Jalan Abu Bakar, 86800 Mersing; tel 07-7991606/fax 07-7993606

White Sand Beach Resort c/o 98 Jalan Harimau Tarum, Century Garden, 80250 Johor Bahru; tel 07-7994995/fax 07-7995279

Pulau Sibu
Sibu Island Cabanas Bsm Sdn Bhd 86800 Mersing; tel 07-3311716/fax 07-3311920

Sibu Island Resort P.O. Box 307, Lot 60-61 ARAS 3, Level Abdullah Ibrahim, Plaza Kota Raya, 80000 Johor Bahru; tel 07-7995555/fax 07-7994455

O & H Kampung Huts c/o #9 Tourist Information Centre, Jalan Abu Bakar, Mersing; tel 07-7993125

Sea Gypsy Village Resort c/o #9 Tourist Information Centre, Jalan Abu Bakar, Mersing; tel 07-2228642/fax 07-2387305

Pulau Rawa
Rawa Safaris Island Resort This popular resort can be booked through: Rawa Safaris Tourist Centre 86800 Mersing; tel 07-7991204/fax 07-7993848

Pulau Tinggi
Nadia's Inn Tropical Resort; tel 07-7995582

Tinggi Island Resort; tel 07-7994461, tel 011-766018

Pulau Aur
Aur Holiday Resort, Kampong Teluk Berhala, Pulau Aur, 86800 Mersing, Johor; tel 07-7995696/fax 07-7994072

Aur Samudra Holiday, Kampong Teluk Sebukan, Pulau Aur, 86800 Mersing, Johor; tel 07-7994217

Pasir Panjang Chalets, Pulau Aur, 86800 Mersing, Johor

Pulau Babi Tengah
More accommodation is planned, but to date the main resort is

Pirate Bay Island Resort tel 07–241911 and 01–762042 (mobile)
Johor Bahru Office:
Suite 243, Johor Tower, 15 Jalan Gereja, 80100 Johor Bahru; tel 07–241911

Pulau Pemanggil
Pemanggil Holiday Heaven, 1030 Kampung Air Merah, 86800 Mersing; tel 07-7994360

WHERE TO EAT

Most of the places to eat are restaurants attached to accommodation. On Pulau Babi Besar try the open-air restaurant at the Radin Island Resort or the cheap-but-good Sundancer II restaurant. Pulau Sibu's O & H Kampung Huts offers great curries alongside Western fare. On the larger islands there can be excellent outdoor food stalls.

DIVE FACILITIES

White Sand Beach Resort c/o 98 Jalan Harimau Tarum, Century Garden, 80250 Johor Bahru; tel 07-7994995/fax 07-7995279

Sibu Island Cabanas Bsm Sdn Bhd 86800 Mersing; tel 07-3311716/fax 07-3311920

FILM PROCESSING

Johor Bahru has several mini-labs for processing print film, E6 processing can be organized by:

Chau Wah Fotografi Sdn Bhd L–4, 72 & 73 Plaza Kotaraya, 80000 Johor Bahru; tel 07–246839

Johor Foto Enterprise G–24 Holiday Plaza, Jalan Dato Sulaiman, 80250 Johor Bahru; tel 07–310463

HOSPITALS

There is a small hospital in Mersing (tel 07–793333). The main hospital in Johor Bahru is:

Hospital Sultanah Aminah tel 07–231666

LOCAL HIGHLIGHTS

For local highlights on the mainland, refer to the directory covering Pahang Marine Parks which lists the main places of interest (page 80). Pulau Sibu offers canoeing and windsurfing (you can hire the relevant craft), and jungle treks are organized across the island; there is also some good walking along the beautiful beaches, although swimmers should beware of the currents. You can take a boat-trip (1hr) to Tanjung Leman, on the mainland about 30km (20 miles) south of Mersing; this tiny village is picturesque, but won't detain you long. Pulau Rawa's Rawa Safaris Island Resort offers canoeing, windsurfing and all sorts of other watersports. Again, the beaches are beautiful. Leatherback Turtles lay their eggs in July on Pulau Babi Tengah. If you get the opportunity, take a boat to Pulau Tinggi, which has a truly splendid beach. More to the point, however, the island is an extinct volcano; climbs up the mountain are pretty strenuous and take 4–5hr (round trip), but are worth it. Don't attempt the climb on your own, because it can be dangerous. A much safer option is to hire a local guide on the island. Other activities offered by Pulau Tinggi include **fishing**, **windsurfing** and **boating**. Pulau Babi Besar is geared to the conventional holidaymaker.

JOHOR BAHRU

Johor Bahru is a modern city and the gateway to Malaysia from the south. Accessed by the 1km (½ mile) causeway over the Johor Straits, the people of Singapore virtually use Johor Bahru as an extension of the island for shopping and eating out. Because of this, the causeway is extremely congested with traffic at weekends.

in the top 15m (50ft) where there are several vertical cracks with the most westerly one forming the so-called tunnel. At 15m (50ft) the cracks end at a terrace of sand and rubble over which the wall plunges into the depths. This site is great for stony corals and among the gorgonians, large sponges and tubastrea corals there are many crustaceans and crinoids, lionfish, bannerfish, pufferfish and batfish while shoals of fusiliers dash about.

2 RUNWAY

★★★★★★★★★

Location: Between the two channels into the lagoon.
Access: By boat.
Conditions: Choppy with moderate to strong currents.
Average depth: 15m (50ft)
Maximum depth: 50m+ (165ft+)
Visibility: Can approach the mythical 60m (200ft).
A steep wall with lots of crevices and gullies sheltering soldierfish, squirrelfish, anthias, groupers and a myriad of other reef fish. However, there is plenty of action off the wall where in the open water there can be shoals of Bigeye Trevally, large tuna, Whitetip Reef Sharks, Grey Reef Sharks and Scalloped Hammerhead Sharks.

3 SNAPPER LEDGE

★★★★★★★★★

Location: West of the old (westernmost) channel.
Access: By boat.
Conditions: Choppy with moderate to strong currents.
Average depth: 150m (50ft)
Maximum depth: 50m+ (165ft+)
Visibility: Can approach the mythical 60m (200ft).
An easy dive with fine corals and a myriad of reef fish though you should regularly look out into the blue where big fish are often seen. Popular with photographers as it is well lit the reef fish include parrotfish, anthias, moray eels, Clown Triggerfish, surgeonfish, butterflyfish, angelfish, Moorish Idols, Bluespotted Ribbontail Rays, Eagle Rays and clownfish in anemones.

4 D' WALL AND SHARKS CAVE

★★★★★

Location: Southeast of the westernmost point.
Access: By boat.
Conditions: Choppy with moderate to strong currents.
Average depth: 30m (100ft)
Maximum depth: 50m+ (165ft+)
Visibility: Can approach the mythical 60m (200ft).
D' Wall is vertical with good coral growth that is only interrupted by a sandy shelf at around 40m (130ft) before plunging into the depths. Littered with large barrel sponges and gorgonian sea fans adorned with multi-coloured feather stars and several species of nudibranch. A good site for finding Bluespotted Ribbontail Rays, Leopard Sharks and Whitetip Reef Sharks resting on the sand. Most species of the local reef fish can be found including anthias, moray eels, Clown Triggerfish, surgeonfish, bannerfish, butterflyfish, Emperor Angelfish, Humphead (Napoleon) Wrasse, Moorish Idols and clownfish in anemones while Eagle Rays and Manta Rays sometimes pass by. Beyond the western end of D' Wall there is Sharks Cave at 25m (80ft) where 'sleeping' Leopard Sharks and Whitetip Reef Sharks and even the occasional Nurse Shark are found. Deeper down it is common to find Grey Reef Sharks and Scalloped Hammerhead Sharks.

5 VALLEY

★★★★★★★★★

Location: The westernmost point.
Access: By boat.
Conditions: Choppy with moderate to strong currents.
Average depth: 20m (65ft)
Maximum depth: 50m+ (165ft+)
Visibility: Can approach the mythical 60m (200ft).
At first this site looks relatively barren when compared with most of the other Layang Layang sites, for the first 20m (65ft) it is a gentle slope with stony corals broken by the surge and then it drops into the deep. However, when you look harder, all the expected reef fish are there and it is a macro photographers' paradise. Crabs, shrimps, lobsters and nudibranchs abound plus Garden Eels, Moray Eels, clownfish in anemones, Humphead (Napoleon) Wrasse, triggerfish guarding their nests, squirrelfish, soldierfish, anthias, angelfish, butterfish and Bluespotted Ribbontail Rays.

Turtles, Manta Rays and Eagle Rays are often seen and Grey Reef, Whitetip Reef and Scalloped Hammerhead Sharks seek out cleaning stations, Thresher Sharks have been spotted.

6 WRASSE STRIP

★★★★★★★★★

Location: Northeast of the westernmost point.
Access: By boat.
Conditions: Choppy with moderate to strong currents.
Average depth: 20m (65ft)
Maximum depth: 50m+ (165ft+)
Visibility: Can approach the mythical 60m (200ft).
Wrasse Strip has everything if you keep your eyes open. A gentle shelf with a rich growth of healthy stony and

soft corals, gorgonians, sponges and clownfish in anemones, the best diving is from the surface to 20m (65ft) with Blacktip Sharks in the open and Whitetip Reef Sharks resting in crevices. Turtles are common, Manta Rays and other fish attend cleaning stations and Giant Clams can be found. The fish life is a grand mixture of reef fish and pelagic fish.

7 CRACK REEF/NAVIGATOR LANE

★★★★★★★★★★★

Location: The northern side of the reef.
Access: By boat.
Conditions: Choppy with moderate to strong currents.
Average depth: 20m (65ft)
Maximum depth: 50m+ (165ft+)
Visibility: Can approach the mythical 60m (200ft).
These two sites are much the same and can be treated either as a multilevel dive, commencing deep down and slowly rising to shallower depths to release nitrogen, or as an entirely shallow water dive. A steep slope drops down to 50m (165ft) before dropping into the depths. There is a coral garden from 5–15m (16–50ft), huge Barrel Sponges, gorgonians of all types including Black Coral and almost every possible reef fish. There are plenty of sea stars, feather stars, sea cucumbers, crabs, lobsters, shrimps and nudibranchs, while lone Scalloped Hammerhead Sharks have been seen at 10m (33ft) with trevallies in their mouths. If you dive to 40m (130ft) there is a narrow cleft with a large gathering of Lionfish (*Pterois volitans*).

8 GORGONIAN FOREST

★★★★★★★★★★

Location: The northeast point.
Access: By boat.
Conditions: Choppy with moderate to strong currents.
Average depth: 30m (100ft)
Maximum depth: 50m+ (165ft+)
Visibility: Can approach the mythical 60m (200ft).
Along with its similar neighbours, this is the most popular and spectacular area of the reef because of the strong currents. A gentle slope to 30m (100ft), which then flattens out as a terrace before plunging into the depths, the site gets its name from the colossal sea fans and whip corals. There are many small crevices and terraces harbouring common reef fish and crustaceans, Bumphead Parrotfish either singly or in large shoals, turtles, Manta Rays and huge Barrel Sponges. Off the wall there are pelagic species, enormous Dogtooth Tuna, barracuda, Humphead (Napoleon) Wrasse, Bigeye Trevallies, Scalloped Hammerhead Sharks, Grey Reef Sharks and smaller groups of Whitetip Reef Sharks.

9 THE POINT

★★★★★

Location: The east point.
Access: By boat.
Conditions: Choppy with moderate to strong currents.
Average depth: 30m (100ft)
Maximum depth: 50m+ (165ft+)
Visibility: Can approach the mythical 60m (200ft).
The actual east point, which bears the brunt of the currents and the aerated water and nutrients that accompany them. Similar to its neighbours Gorgonian Forest, Dogtooth Lair and Wreck Point, for experienced divers this is probably the best dive on Layang-Layang.

10 DOGTOOTH LAIR

★★★★★

Location: Southwest of the east point.
Access: By boat.
Conditions: Choppy with moderate to strong currents.
Average depth: 30m (100ft)
Maximum depth: 50m+ (165ft+)
Visibility: Can approach the mythical 60m (200ft).
Again this brilliant dive site is very similar to its neighbours. The name comes from the large, some would say barrel-size Dogtooth Tuna that are regularly seen.

11 WRECK POINT

★★★★★★★★★★

Location: Just east of the new channel by the concrete wall.
Access: By boat.
Conditions: Choppy with moderate to strong currents.
Average depth: 15m (50ft)
Maximum depth: 50m+ (165ft+)
Visibility: Can approach the mythical 60m (200ft).
Either used as the final out-gassing stop for the previous three dives or as an easier shallow dive in its own right, Wreck Point is named after an old wreck that nowadays is just a few scraps of iron on the seabed. Sloping gently to 15m (50ft) the reef then plunges into the depths with shoals of Dogtooth Tuna and barracuda and a larger shoal of Bigeye Trevallies along the wall. There are coral gardens that include Lettuce coral, mushrooms of Porites corals, huge Barrel Sponges and Black Corals and other gorgonians at medium depths, anemones with clownfish, several Giant Clams and hundreds of species of reef fish and Whitetip Reef Sharks at shallower depths, while Grey Reef and Scalloped Hammerhead sharks often appear.

HOW TO GET THERE

Kota Kinabalu is easily accessible by international flights from Kuala Lumpur, Hong Kong, Manila, Singapore, Bangkok, Brunei, Taipei and Seoul. It is also the take-off hub for flights to Tawau, Sandakan, Labuan and Kuching (Sarawak). The airport is 7km (4 miles) from the city centre.

Flights with small STOL aircraft are organized through the resort.

WHERE TO STAY

The only accommodation available on the island is:

Layang Layang Island Resort, Kuala Lumpur Sales Office, Letter Box 12, Block A, Ground Floor, A-0-3, Megan Phileo Avenue, 12 Jalan Yap Kwan Seng, 50450 Kuala Lumpur; tel 03-21622877/fax 03-21622980; e-mail layang@pop.jaring.my; www.layanglayang.com. Now upgraded to 82 rooms and 4 suites with air conditioning and en-suite facilities. The resort is closed from November to March.

DIVE FACILITIES

Layang Layang Island Resort have the only facilities on the island.

FILM PROCESSING

ScubaZoo Images operate E6 processing at Layang Layang when regular tourist numbers are high enough:

ScubaZoo Images, PO Box 20149, Pejabat Pos Luyang, 88758 Kota Kinabalu, Sabah; tel 088–232068/fax 088-237068; email info@scubazoo.com; www.scubazoo.com

Kota Kinabalu and Wisma Merdeka has numerous mini-labs. For reliable E6 transparency processing use the following: **Ban Loong Color Foto Centre** AG52, Ground Floor, Wisma Merdeka, PO Box 12064, 88822 Kota Kinabalu, Sabah; tel 088–217950

HOSPITALS

Queen Elizabeth Hospital 88586 Kota Kinabalu; tel 088–218166/fax 088–211999

Health and Paramedic Service PO Box 11201, 88813 Kota Kinabalu; tel 088–50555/fax 088–221248

LOCAL HIGHLIGHTS

The great thing about Layang-Layang is that the island is unspoilt! The corollary of this is that there is a dearth of things to do other than diving, fishing, kayaking, windsurfing and bird-watching.

Pickhandle Barracuda (Sphyraena jello). Immature barracudas school in large shoals of 500-1000. Adults tend to swim singly and can become dangerous.

DIVING AND SNORKELLING TIPS

• All snorkelling and diving equipment should be rinsed with fresh water after use and dried off in the shade.

• Never leave equipment out in the tropical sun.

• For snorkelling or diving you can buy waterproof marine identification cards and waterproof books which will tell you what you are looking at underwater.

• A mesh bag is handy for carrying your kit around. When you've finished snorkelling you can simply dip the whole lot in a rinse tank or bath but you must not rinse a regulator in this way.

• If you get cramp in your calf muscles or instep, reach forward and grab the end of your fin with one hand and straighten your leg while pulling the fin towards you. If the cramp is at the front of the leg, reach behind rather than forwards and pull the fin up and back.

• You don't need a weight belt for free diving unless you are wearing a wetsuit or are obese, in either of which cases your buoyancy will be greater than normal so that you find it harder to descend.

SABAH
NORTHWEST COAST

The second largest state in Malaysia after Sarawak, Sabah's name came from the Arabic Zir-e Bad, meaning 'The Land Below the Wind', that refers to its position just below the typhoon belt. While Sarawak's chief characteristics are rainforests and rivers, Sabah is identified with mountains — in particular, the Crocker Range in the northwest region, which is dominated by Mount Kinabalu 4101m (13,455ft).

KOTA KINABALU

The focal point of Sabah's northwest coast is Kota Kinabalu, the state capital. Since the settlement was first established here as Jesselton by the British in 1883 (it was renamed in 1963) it has experienced a turbulent history, with pirates, rebellions and fires. It was completely destroyed by the Allies during World War II in order to stop the Japanese being able to use it as a base, but was later rebuilt mostly on reclaimed land in Gaya Bay.

Some time ago the northwest coast of Sabah was more generously endowed with beautiful coral reefs but, with a relatively high population density for the region, the reefs have suffered from siltation, destructive fishing methods and coral quarrying for construction.

MARINE PARKS

Tunku Abdul Rahman Marine Park is very close to Kota Kinabalu, so it gets crowded at weekends and during holiday periods. Tiga Park is more difficult to reach and is often quite empty of visitors, but it has only two real dive sites. Further south, off Labuan Federal Territory, the corals suffer from river run-off and siltation, but there is excellent wreck diving. Except for Labuan, this is not an area you would normally consider visiting specifically for its diving – especially as some of the best diving in the world is only a short flight away, at Pulau Sipadan on the east coast (see page 130). Since the water is relatively shallow, the visibility is soon spoilt by any windy weather. However, if you happen to be in the area anyway and the weather is fine, then bear in mind that the diving is very easy to get to and perfect for the training of novices.

Opposite: *The idyllic Sapi Island in the Tunku Abdul Rahman Marine Park.*
Above: *The Copperband Butterfly (Chelmon rostratus), common on silty inner reefs and wrecks.*

Tunku Abdul Rahman Marine Park

Lying 3–8km (2–5 miles) off Kota Kinabalu, the Tunku Abdul Rahman Marine Park consists of five islands: Pulau Gaya, Pulau Sapi, Pulau Manukan, Pulau Mamutik and Pulau Sulug. They are covered with lowland tropical rainforest; this is still undisturbed primary forest on Pulau Gaya within the park area, but on the other islands it is mostly secondary. These rainforest areas are home to a variety of interesting flora and fauna. Pulau Gaya, at 1483ha (3665 acres) by far the largest of the group – with a highest peak rising to 305m (1000ft) – is worth visiting just for the wildlife.

In 1974 most of Pulau Gaya and all of Pulau Sapi were declared the Tunku Abdul Rahman Marine Park, leaving only the small fishing village on the eastern promontory of Pulau Gaya out of the park (it remains so to this day). In 1979 the nearby Pulau Manukan, Pulau Mamutik and Pulau Sulug were added to the park.

ACCESS

All the islands can be reached by a 20min boat or ferry ride from the jetty by the Hyatt Kinabalu International Hotel, the Tanjung Aru Resort or the Kinabalu Yacht Club. This easy accessibility makes the islands very popular with local day-trippers at weekends. August is the high season for local holidays. There is an entrance fee to visit the islands on land.

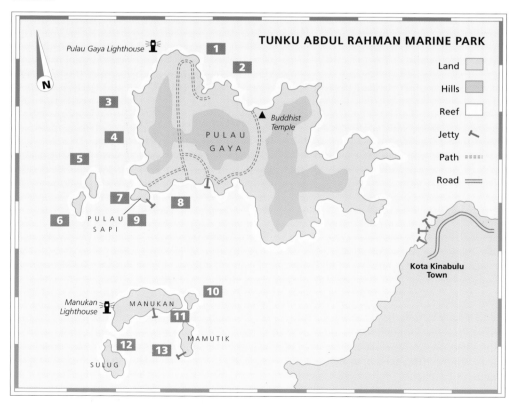

SHALLOW REEFS

The north and west shores of the islands have been ravaged by monsoon weather, so that there are rocky cliffs and banks of rubble, but the eastern and southern shores have golden beaches slowly shelving to reefs. These reefs are generally shallow, and most have been damaged by blast-fishing in the past, but where they are still intact they offer a profusion of brightly coloured stony corals, some of which are quite big.

THE CORAL

The corals are predominantly stony; in particular, there are large areas of colourful staghorn coral and large table corals (*Acropora*), there is lettuce coral, and (good news for snorkellers) very little fire coral. In among the larger corals are smaller areas of brain coral, mushroom corals, whip corals, bubble coral, blue and yellow sea squirts, sponges and large brown vase sponges. Also present are large blue sea stars, smaller green sea stars and cushion stars. Several colour varieties of feather stars are common in daylight, and there are lots of Christmas Tree Worms and fan worms.

FISH FAUNA

The fish fauna is more limited, but all the smaller reef fish can be seen, and there are quite large shoals of fusiliers; several varieties of anemones act as hosts to clownfish. Crabs and shells are still found, but very few lobsters. Whale Sharks can be seen here from January to April.

The Blue-spotted Ribbontail Ray (Taeniura lymma), often camouflages its bright colours by covering itself in sand.

SURPRISE ROCK ISLAND

It is hard to equate modern Borneo with volcanic activity but all the signs are present: there are hot springs at Poring and active mud volcanoes in the Tiga and Turtle Islands parks, Pulau Sipadan is the result of volcanic uplift, and Mount Kinabalu, the youngest granite pluton in the world, is still rising by 5mm (0.2in) per year.

On 15 April 1988 local fishermen were startled when a new island, almost as big as a football pitch, was thrust up out of the sea 14km (9 miles) east of Pulau Banggi off the northern tip of Sabah, close to Philippines territorial waters. The nearby islanders named it Pulau Batu Hairan ('Surprise Rock Island'). Pulau Batu Hairan must have been quite a sight, with all its beautiful stony coral formations standing proud before they collapsed.

In fact, this area has been thrust up twice before during this century, first in 1914 and again in 1942. Unfortunately, in 1988 as before, the seabed was not thrust up far enough for the island to survive, and Pulau Batu Hairan was soon reclaimed by the waves.

BULIJONG BAY

The major beach area on Pulau Gaya is at Bulijong Bay, known locally as Police Beach because it used to be used by the police for target practice! This area has a 400m (440yd) beach with excellent swimming and some good snorkelling either side of the bay. It can get very busy, so most foreign visitors prefer the more secluded beaches on the smaller islands. There are forest trails and mangrove trails on board walks.

PULAU SAPI

Pulau Sapi, adjacent to the southwest tip of Pulau Gaya, is a small island – 10ha (25 acres) – with one of the best beaches in the park. It has most of the public facilities you would hope for, but no accommodation. You can camp if you have written permission from the Sabah Parks Office in Kota Kinabalu or from the park warden. There is a nature trail, and glass-bottomed boats are available for people who want to view the coral reef without getting wet. To the southeast there is good snorkelling.

> ### PECULIAR BIRDS
>
> Tunku Abdul Rahman Marine Park is home to a bizarre bird called the Megapode (*Megapodus freycinet*).
>
> This bird incubates its eggs by burying them in mounds of sand and leaves; the leaves ferment like a compost heap and produce enough warmth to incubate the eggs until they are ready to hatch. A single mound may be used by several birds. The birds constantly tend the mound to control temperature. Now rarely found on Western Sabah's coast, the Megapode survives in small populations on all the islands in the Park except Pulau Mamutik; it is also found on the larger of Pulau Tiga Park's islands, further south.
>
> Other birdlife on the Tunku Abdul Rahman Marine Park islands includes large species such as the White-bellied Sea Eagle, Green Heron and Pied Hornbill, as well as smaller and commoner species like sunbirds, flycatchers, Pink-necked Green Pigeon and sandpipers.

PULAU MANUKAN

Pulau Manukan covers 21ha (51 acres), and has the Park Headquarters. There are furnished chalets for rent, a swimming pool, football field, tennis and squash courts and a restaurant; the accommodation has to be booked through the Sabah Parks Office in Kota Kinabalu. Good snorkelling is to be had on the west, north and south coasts.

PULAU MAMUTIK

Pulau Mamutik is the smallest island – 6ha (15 acres) – and the nearest to the mainland. It has good beaches, but the one on the eastern side, facing Tanjung Aru, slopes down steeply. The island has a rest house, water and electricity, but you must bring your own food.

PULAU SULUG

Pulau Sulug, the island furthest away from Kota Kinabalu, is relatively undeveloped, though there are some picnic shelters and toilets. At its eastern extremity is a long sand-spit and a beach; apart from this the island is rocky. It is popular with foreign tourists, who like the quiet, uncrowded atmosphere. There is good snorkelling at the island's southern end.

The wettest months in this region are during the southwest monsoon period, June to December, while the driest months are January to May. The best time for diving is April to August, with the calmest weather being in February to May. The sites described below are all in warm shallow waters. They can be dived in bad weather, but the stirred-up sand renders visibility almost zero; otherwise, at all the sites the average visibility is about 10m (33ft). The depths given are for high tide.

OTHER ISLANDS

Other islands to which diving trips are possible include Pulau Mantanani and Pulau Mengalum. There is a resort, Borneo Sea Adventure's Pulau Mantanani Resort on Mantanani, an hour's boat ride by speedboat from the mainland northwest of Kota Belud.

1 PULAU GAYA: BULIJONG BAY

★★

Location: 500m (550yd) east of the northeast point of Bulijong Bay.
Access: By small boat to the east of the northeast end of the bay until the reef is visible.
Conditions: Some gentle currents, depending on the tide. Visibility is quickly ruined by windy weather.
Average depth: 10m (33ft)
Maximum depth: 21m (70ft)
A long gentle slope from 5m (16ft) to 21m (70ft) goes out to the north. There are table and staghorn corals, boulder corals, encrusting corals and sponges, blue sea stars, black sea urchins, nudibranchs, flat worms and small reef fish.
    You can snorkel off the central section of the west side of Bulijong Bay.

2 PULAU GAYA: MERANGIS REEF

★★

Location: 400m (440yd) northeast of the eastern tip of Bulijong Bay.
Access: By small boat out to the east until the reef is visible.
Conditions: Calm in good weather; possibly some swell and surge as the tide changes.
Average depth: 9m (30ft)
Maximum depth: 26m (85ft)
A tongue slopes out in line with the promontory. The best diving is on the east side, but there is more marine life on the end, where a short wall drops to 26m (85ft). The site has table and staghorn corals, boulder and brain corals, encrusting corals and sponges, nudibranchs, sea stars, sea urchins and small reef fish.
    You can snorkel off the north end of the promontory.

3 PULAU GAYA: AGILL REEF

★★

Location: At the centre of the west side of Pulau Gaya.
Access: By boat.
Conditions: Generally calm; possibly some swell and surge as the tide changes.
Average depth: 15m (50ft)
Maximum depth: 26m (85ft)
On a gentle slope from 8m (25ft) to 26m (85ft) are table, staghorn and boulder corals, with Christmas Tree Worms, brain corals, encrusting corals and sponges, sea anemones and small reef fish.

4 PULAU GAYA: CLEMENT REEF

★★★

Location: West–northwest of the gap between Pulau Sapi and Pulau Gaya.
Access: By boat.
Conditions: Generally calm; possibly some swell and surge as the tide turns.
Average depth: 15m (50ft)
Maximum depth: 26m (85ft)
A gentle slope from 8m (25ft) to 26m (85ft) has good large table, staghorn, lettuce, brain and boulder corals, encrusting corals and sponges, Christmas Tree Worms and fan worms, and vase and small barrel sponges. There are plenty of small reef fish, cuttlefish, catfish, sea urchins, sea stars, cushion stars and nudibranchs, lionfish, scorpionfish, stonefish and some groupers.

5 NORTH EDGELL PATCH
6 SOUTH EDGELL PATCH

★★

Location: West of Pulau Sapi.
Access: By small boat west from the island until the patch reefs are visible.
Conditions: Generally calm; possibly some swell and surge as the tide changes.
Average depth: 15m (50ft)
Maximum depth: 20m (65ft)
There is a gentle slope from 9m (30ft) to 20m (65ft). Both of these sites have been badly damaged by blast-fishing, leaving lots of coral rubble coated in encrusting coral, sponges and algae. There are small varieties of reef fish, black sea urchins, sea stars, cushion stars, sea cucumbers and nudibranchs. The two sites are open to the ocean, so there are occasional pelagic visitors, including Manta Rays.

ISLAND FORMATION

Geologically the islands of the Tunku Abdul Rahman Marine Park are part of the Crocker range, which stretches from the northern end of Sabah right down to the border with Sarawak. The islands were formed towards the end of the last ice age when rising sea levels isolated them from the mainland. The underlying sandstone of which they are formed can easily be seen around their coastlines, with outcrops sculpted by the weather into caves, honeycombs and deep crevasses.

7 PULAU SAPI: SOUTHWEST REEF

★★

Location: Off the southwest promontory of Pulau Sapi.
Access: By small boat to the west of the promontory.
Conditions: Generally calm; possibly some swell and surge as the tide turns.
Average depth: 6m (20ft) to 9m (30ft)
Maximum depth: 17m (56ft)
This site offers shallow diving in very easy conditions – ideal for novices.

8 PULAU SAPI: SAPI REEF

★★★★★★

Location: Off the southeast corner of Pulau Sapi.
Access: By boat.
Conditions: Generally calm; possibly some swell and surge as the tide turns.
Average depth: 9m (30ft)
Maximum depth: 17m (56ft)
Shallow diving in very easy conditions with table, staghorn, boulder, bubble and brain corals, encrusting corals and sponges, Christmas Tree Worms, fan worms, sea stars, cushion stars, sea cucumbers, sea squirts and sea urchins. There are lots of small reef fish, catfish, cuttlefish, lionfish, scorpionfish, stonefish, nudibranchs, flat worms and colourful feather stars. When the shallow water is surging it is quite difficult to achieve any good close-up photography of the smaller creatures.

There is quite good snorkelling off this corner of Pulau Sapi.

9 PULAU SAPI: RON REEF

★★★★★★

Location: South of Pulau Sapi.
Access: By boat.
Conditions: Generally calm; possibly some swell and surge as the tide changes.
Average depth: 9m (30ft)
Maximum depth: 17m (56ft)
Shallow diving in very easy conditions with boulders; the reef life and fish fauna are much the same as for the Sapi Reef (Site 8) including table, staghorn, boulder, bubble and brain corals, encrusting corals and sponges, Christmas Tree worms, fan worms, sea stars, cushion stars, sea cucumbers, sea squirts, sea urchins and many species of smaller reef fish.

The surging waters pose the same difficulties for close-up photography.

10 PULAU MANUKAN: MID REEF

★★★★

Location: Directly east of the east point of Pulau Manukan.
Access: By boat.
Conditions: Some light current, with swell and surge as the tide turns.
Average depth: 9m (30ft)
Maximum depth: 20m (65ft)
A gentle slope from 6m (20ft) to 20m (65ft) with few soft corals but lots of table, staghorn, lettuce, bubble, boulder and brain corals, encrusting corals and sponges, vase sponges and some small whip corals. There are Christmas Tree and fan worms, nudibranchs and flat worms, sea squirts, sea stars, cushion stars, black sea urchins, sea cucumbers and lots of feather stars, as well as lionfish, scorpionfish, stonefish and shoals of small parrotfish, catfish, sweepers and fusiliers. Although anemones are frequent, few of them have attendant clownfish. Barracuda, groupers and turtles are common.

11 PULAU MANUKAN: MANUKAN REEF

★★★

Location: East-southeast of the southeast corner of Pulau Manukan.
Access: By boat from the southeast corner of Pulau Manukan towards Pulau Mamutik.
Conditions: Some currents and heavy boat traffic.
Average depth: 10m (33ft)
Maximum depth: 20m (65ft)
The site offers a gentle slope from 5m (16ft) to 20m (65ft). Small turtles and barracuda are often seen.

There tends to be heavy boat traffic here, so **this site is definiteley not for snorkellers or for novices**, who might have trouble maintaining correct buoyancy and possibly float up when boats were passing. There is, however, good snorkelling off the north and south shores of Pulau Manukan.

12 PULAU SULUG: SULUG REEF

★★★★

Location: East of the beach and the north promontory of Pulau Sulug.
Access: By boat from north of Pulau Sulug.
Conditions: Some current and swell.
Average depth: 9m (30ft)
Maximum depth: 26m (85ft)
A tongue heading out east, with the best diving on the

and small crabs and cuttlefish as well as one anemone, Coeloplana, hide among the spines of long-spined sea urchins. Trumpetfish often hide in whip corals, and various crabs and shrimps and the Longnose Hawkfish conceal themselves amongst gorgonian sea fans of the same colour as themselves.

CLOWNFISH AND ANEMONES

But the best known marine partnership is that shared by clownfish (and some other dam-selfish) with sea anemones. The fish are more correctly called Anemonefish, but most divers and aquarists call them clownfish because of their gaudy colours and apparently eccentric behaviour as they charge, snap and grunt at other fish, at divers and even at their own reflection in a diver's mask. The origins of this behaviour are in fact largely territorial.

A SAFE HAVEN

The anemone gives the clownfish a haven to which it can retreat if threatened by predators and also provides it with a food source supple-mentary to its principal diet of floating zoo-plankton or algae growing nearby. The clown-fish's scavenging of food scraps, algae and parasites within the anemone helps keep the latter clean and healthy, and the movement of

the clownfish creates a respiratory current within the anemone. Clownfish have even been known to bring the anemone food, although it is not proven behaviour in the wild. Nevertheless, the clownfish would seem to get more out of the partnership than the anemone in that, while clownfish apparently cannot sur-vive for long without a host anemone, anemones can thrive without clownfish.

ANEMONE STING

Anemones, which in areas of high water movement can grow to be over 1m (40in) across, have other symbiotes, algae called zooxanthellae. They catch passing food with their sticky mucus and can kill live prey using the stinging nematocysts in their tentacles, but most of their nutrient comes from the symbiot-ic algae. Clownfish are not immune to the sting; however, the anemone's mucus contains chemicals that counter the sting, stopping each tentacle from stinging any of the others, or even itself, and the clownfish coat themselves in this. They also have a thick mucus layer which they generate themselves for protection.

Other small damselfish, notably the Domino Damselfish *Dascyllus trimaculatus*, can occupy anemones during their juvenile phase.

Richardsons Clownfish (Amphiprion rubrocinctus) with Radianthus anemone. The partnership is of benefit to both, though the clownfish has greater dependence.

Closed anemone, Radianthus ritteri, now known as Heteractis magnifica, with a Clownfish Amphiprion ocellaris, also known as Common Clownfish or Clown Anemonefish.

Pulau Tiga Park

Located 48km (30 miles) southwest of Kota Kinabalu, in Kimanis Bay, the Pulau Tiga National Park, gazetted in 1978, comprises Pulau Tiga and the two smaller islands Pulau Kalampunian Damit and Pulau Kalampunian Besar. Its total area is 15,864ha (39,200 acres).

PULAU TIGA

Now notorious as the film set for the reality television series *Survivor*, Pulau Tiga itself is a beautiful place heavily wooded with dipterocarp forest down to coconut palms at the beach edge. There are park rangers *in situ*, plus on the south of the island, a well laid-out campsite and picnic and barbecue areas along the fine white sandy beaches. The best time for diving is April to August, with the calmest weather being in February to May.

CORAL REEFS

The reefs off the two smaller islands and the north side of Pulau Tiga are heavily blast-fished, although there are two good dive sites to the south. All over, there are small table, lettuce, boulder and brain corals, antler-shaped corals and encrusting corals and sponges. Most of the stony corals are damaged and covered in silt, but in many places small soft corals thrive.

SNORKELLING

The park is noted for having more gorgonians and whip corals than normally found on Sabah's west coast. Visibility in this region is generally about 10m (33ft). You could snorkel out from the nearest point on the beach to both of the Picnic Beach dive sites described below but, if the tide reversed, it could be difficult to snorkel back against the current.

1 SOUTH OF THE NORTHWEST END OF PICNIC BEACH

★★★★★★

Location: On Pulau Tiga, 80m (90yd) south of Picnic Beach's northwest corner.
Access: By boat or by snorkelling from the beach.
Conditions: Current, some swell and difficult surge.
Average depth: 9m (30ft)
Maximum depth: 17m (56ft)
Here you find a 30° slope from 4m (13ft) to 17m (56ft) with, despite all the coral debris from blast-fishing, a good fish fauna, especially in the deeper water. There are lettuce corals, brain corals, mushroom corals and boulder corals with Christmas Tree worms, although few table corals. Also present are some gorgonian sea fans – reaching 1m (40in) across – several whip corals, yellow sea squirts, blue tube sponges, blue sea stars and several anemones (lacking attendant clownfish). The fish life includes many small butterflyfish, catfish, small parrotfish, scorpionfish, lionfish, stonefish, surgeonfish and some groupers.

2 SOUTH OF THE SOUTHWEST END OF PICNIC BEACH

★★★

Location: On Pulau Tiga, 80m (90yd) south of Picnic Beach's southwest corner.
Access: By boat or by snorkelling from the beach.
Conditions: Current, some swell and difficult surge.
Average depth: 9m (30ft)
Maximum depth: 17m (56ft)
A gentle slope falls westward from 6m (20ft) to 17m (56ft). There is much coral rubble from blast-fishing but, even so, lots of small fish swim among good table and brain corals, whip corals, small soft corals and tiny gorgonian sea fans. There are congregations of black sea urchins, several cuttlefish, nudibranchs, sea cucumbers, shoals of small parrotfish and fusiliers, yellow sea squirts, blue tube sponges, big clams, Christmas-tree Worms, fan worms and anemones (most lacking attendant clownfish).

Previous page: *Sunset seen from Pulau Tiga Park, off the west coast of Sabah, Malaysia.*
Below: *Large Barrel Sponges (Petrosia sp.) can grow up to 2m (6¹/₂ft) and are extremely common in the Pacific.*

use alkaline batteries in your back-up light. Small `Q light' torches make good, cheap back-up lights (or even as main lights), and photographers can also use them as focusing lights.

A wrist lanyard is another good idea: it will keep your torch conveniently nearby if you drop it, or if you need a spare hand for anything. Divers often keep a chemical light-stick attached to their cylinder or weight-belt so they can be easily found if their torches fail.

FLOODLIGHTS

Some resorts and boats set floodlights over the water so that clients above water can watch the antics of fish, octopuses and cuttlefish. However, these lights also attract hordes of small biting creatures to the surface. Swimming through these swarms can be uncomfortable, to say the least.

DANGERS

The dangers of night diving and snorkelling are not sharks, which are rarely seen at night, but more familiar creatures. While your vision is limited by the range and breadth of your torchlight it is easy to brush against organisms you would normally avoid, like fire coral, lionfish, stinging hydroids, spiny urchins,

> ### NIGHT DIVING TIPS
>
> - Avoid dangling equipment that will snag.
> - Tuck your contents gauge into your belt where you can easily find it when you want to read it.
> - Set yourself a diving time – for example, 30min out and 30min back. Alternatively, set yourself to turn round when your contents gauge has depleted by one-third.
> - Do not try to cover long distances.
> - Take your time, so that you can peer into nooks and crannies to see the small creatures there.
> - Ensure you have warm dry clothing and a hot drink waiting for when you come out of the water.

scorpionfish and stonefish. In fact, scorpionfish often get their camouflage wrong, so that they are easily seen bright red in the torchlight, but stonefish are even more difficult to see at night than they are during the day, often giving themselves away only by moving.

Opposite: *Darkband Fusilier (Pterocaesio tile), the most wide-ranging and often the most common of fusiliers, showing night-time coloration.*

Below: *Divers prepare for a night dive. Underwater exploration by torchlight can reveal a world hidden from sight during the day.*

SABAH: EAST/SOUTHEAST COAST

Eastern Sabah is less mountainous than the western part of the state and has traditionally been a land of cocoa and timber. However, in recent times world cocoa prices have fallen and eastern Sabah's timber is running out, so much of the land is now being made over to the cultivation of oil palms. This area borders a dissident muslim area of the Philippines. There were pirate raids for monetary gain in the 1970s and early '80s, but recently Abu Sayyaf guerrillas seized tourists from two dive resorts. The Malaysian government has since increased its navy patrols and police presence considerably.

SANDAKAN

The region's biggest town is Sandakan, which used to be the state capital and was hugely prosperous because of the timber trade – at one time it was said to have more millionaires than anywhere else in the world. Due to its wealth and the large number of Chinese traders who settled here, it became known as Sabah's Hong Kong. All that changed at the end of World War II, when the town was flattened by Allied bombing. Soon afterwards the capital was transferred to Kota Kinabalu (then called Jesselton). But today Sandakan is thriving once again, exporting logs, palm oil and swiftlets' nests for use in making birds'-nest soup; it is also Malaysia's biggest fishing port and a major exporter of frozen prawns and other seafood.

To the visitor, Sandakan is the gateway to the Turtle Islands Park, the Kinabatangan River and the Sepilok Orang-utan Sanctuary, one of only three in the world — the other two are in Sarawak and Sumatra, respectively. Another gateway is Tawau, previously known for logging and for cocoa estates: it is through Tawau that you reach the world-class diving at Pulau Sipadan and Pulau Sangalaki.

TRAVEL

Most visitors go by air between Kota Kinabalu, Sandakan and Tawau, since the road system in the region cannot be described as good. Moreover, there are numerous government road blocks where visitors travelling overland can encounter difficulties.

Opposite: *A beautiful tropical island off Semporna, on the east coast of Sabah, Malaysia.*
Above: *Hawksbill Turtle (Eretmochelys imbricata). This is the smallest of the marine turtle species.*

Turtle Islands Park

Turtle Islands Park lies close to the Philippines border, 40km (25 miles) north of Sandakan, and comprises three islands: Pulau Selingan, Pulau Gulisan and Pulau Bakkungan Kecil. The park was gazetted in 1977 to protect the Green and Hawksbill Turtles that lay eggs on the beaches here. Green Turtles (*Chelonia mydas*) make up 80% of the turtles in the park, with Pulau Selingan their preferred island for nesting. Hawksbill Turtles (*Eretmochelys imbricata*) prefer Pulau Gulisan. The turtles nest all year round, but the peak season for Green Turtles is August–October and that for Hawksbill Turtles February–April.

PULAU SELINGAN

On Pulau Selingan, the second largest island in the group – 8ha (20 acres) – lantanas grow under coconut palms. The main turtle beaches are on the east side of the island and on the southwest side near to the lighthouse beach; most of the northern shore is rocky. The beaches shelve off as sandy bottoms with some sea grasses; they are good for swimming but not for snorkelling.

TURTLE ISLANDS PARK CHRONOLOGY
• **1966 (1 August):** Malaysia's first turtle hatchery, financed by the Government, established on Pulau Selingan.
• **1971:** The Sabah government compulsorily buys the privately owned Pulau Selingan, Pulau Bakkungan Kecil and Pulau Gulisan for 89,000 ringgits.
• **1972:** The three islands are constituted as game and bird sanctuaries under the Forestry Department
• **1977:** The government converts the three islands, plus the surrounding coral reefs and the seas between the islands, into a 1740-ha (4300-acre) Marine Park.

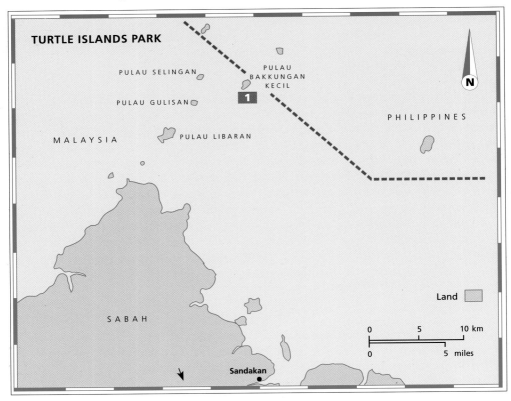

ACCOMMODATION

Pulau Selingan is the only island with accommodation: three multiple-room chalets (somewhat in need of repairs). For fresh water, rain is collected in tanks, and there is only intermittent electricity. There is also an information centre cum restaurant, which is in better condition, plus a ranger station and a turtle hatchery.

Pulau Bakkungan Kecil, the largest island – 8.5ha (21 acres) – is also the one closest to the Philippines border; it has a wide promontory to the southeast. Unlike the other two islands it boasts a small hill at its centre, with active mud volcanoes. The island has coconut palms over lalang grass. There are staff quarters for the hatchery.

Pulau Gulisan, the smallest island – only 1.6ha (4 acres) – is again covered in coconut palms and lalang grass.

Green Turtle (Chelonia mydas) returning to the sea at dawn after laying her eggs.

1 PULAU BAKKUNGAN KECIL: SOUTHERN END

★★★

Location: 100m (110yd) west from the southern end of Pulau Bakkungan Kecil.
Access: By boat (10min) from the accommodation on Pulau Selingan; you may be charged an extra 10 ringgits.
Conditions: Calm; average visibility about 20m (50ft).
Average depth: 1m (40in)
Maximum depth: 1.5m (5ft)

A stony coral garden that is as good as those at Pulau Sipadan (see page 130). There are good blue, green and yellow staghorn corals, large table corals, lots of blue sea stars, black sea cucumbers, salps, Chevron Butterflyfish, parrotfish, damselfish and shoals of fusiliers and catfish.

MAGANGS

En route to Pulau Selingan, in Sandakan Bay, you can see hundreds of *magangs*. These fish-traps, set in 12m (40ft) of water, consist of a bamboo framework supporting fine mesh nets. They are submerged at night, and kerosene lamps are lit on the framework above the water. The main catch is Whitebait.

HOW TO GET THERE

Kota Kinabalu to Sandakan is a 50min flight by Malaysian Airlines. At Sandakan you transfer to the main jetty, where you pick up a small speedboat for the 1hr 20min ride to Pulau Selingan. If you have not already arranged a boat you can fix one up through the local agents or barter at the jetty.

HELICOPTER SERVICE

Kota Kinabalu
Sabah Air Pte Ltd Sabah Air Building, Locked Bag 113, Old Airport Road, 88999 Kota Kinabalu; tel 088–251326; e-mail sabair@tm.net.my; www.borneo-online.com.my/sabahair/corp_info.htm

Tawau
Sabah Air Pte Ltd Locked Bag 15, Tawau Airport, 91009 Tawau; tel 089–774005

Sandakan
Sabah Air Pte Ltd, Sabah Air Hangar Locked Bag 56, Sandakan Airport, 90009 Sandakan; tel 089–660527/fax 089–660545 (payload limit 425kg; 935 pounds)

WHERE TO STAY

Accommodation on Pulau Selingan has to be organized on the mainland through

Park Warden Regional Office East Coast Parks 9th Floor, Wisma Khoo Siak Chew, P.O. Box 768, 90008 Sandakan; tel 089–273453/fax 089–274718
Postal Address:
PO Box 768, Sandakan

You can do this direct or use one of the tour agents listed on page 127.

Sandakan
Upper Price Range
Sandakan Renaissance Hotel P.O. Box 275, Mile 1, Jalan Utara, 90007 Sandakan; tel 089–213299/fax 089–271271; www.renaissancehotels.com/sdkrn

Medium Price Range
Hotel Hsiang Garden Hsiang Garden Estate, Mile 1.5, Jalan Leila, Sandakan; tel 089–273122/fax 089–273127

Hotel Ramai Kilometre 1.5, Jalan Leila Sandakan; tel 089–273222/fax 089–271884

Hotel Nak P.O. Box 761, Jalan Pelabuhan Lama, Sandakan; tel 089–272988/fax 089–272879

City View Hotel Lot 1, Block 23, 3rd Avenue, Sandakan; tel 089–271122/fax 089–273115

Hung Wing Hotel, Jalan Tiga, Sandakan; tel 089–218855/fax 089–18895

Uncle Tan's (see address on page 127).

Convenient for the Sepilok Orang-utan Rehabilitation Centre:

Sepilok Nature Resort 2.5km Sepilok Road @ 22.5km Labuk Road, Sandakan; tel 089–535001/fax 089–535002; e-mail sepilok@po.jaring.my; www.sipadan-resort.com

WHERE TO EAT

Sandakan is famous for inexpensive and delicious seafood; cuisines include Chinese, Indonesian/Malay and Indian Muslim, and you can also find Western, Japanese and Korean food. Try the **Ming Restaurant** in the Renaissance Hotel and the restaurant in the City View Hotel (addresses above), as well as:

XO Steak House Hsiang Garden Estate (opposite Hsiang Garden Hotel), Mile 1.5, Jalan Leila; tel 089–215510. Good selection of Western-style grilled and barbecued Australian Steak, plus seafood.

Seoul Garden Korean Restaurant Hsiang Garden Estate, Mile 1.5, Jalan Leila; tel 089–43891

DIVE FACILITIES

The nearest dive-shop is in Tawau and the nearest diving facilities are those of the Pulau Sipadan operators (see page 138).

FILM PROCESSING

There are several mini-labs for print film in Sandakan. E6 processing can be organized by **Sandakan Photo** on Jalan Dua.

HOSPITALS

Queen Elizabeth Hospital
88586 Kota Kinabalu; tel 088–218166/fax 088–211999

Health and Paramedic Service
PO Box 11201, 88813 Kota Kinabalu; tel 088–50555/fax 088–221248

LOCAL HIGHLIGHTS

It is well worth spending at least half a day looking around Sandakan town. The ornate Chinese temple of **Pui Gisin** is the largest in Sabah. The people of **Bajau water village**, the oldest village in Sandakan, are friendly and like being photographed. Other places worth going to include the house of **Agnes Newton Keith** (author of *The Land Below the Wind* [1939] and of various books describing life under the Japanese occupation), the **mosque** and the stone **Church of St Michael's of All Angels**. There is a **crocodile farm** at 8 Labuk Road, near the airport.
The **Sepilok Orangutan Rehabilitation Centre**, 25km (15 miles; 30min) outside Sandakan, is a must. Umbrellas/raincoats and mosquito repellent are useful. Feeding times are 10:00

LANKAYAN DIVE RESORT

North of the Turtle Islands, deep in the Sulu Sea near to the Philippines, Pulau Sipadan Resort & Tours have constructed a resort on Lankayan Island. The island has been uninhabited for long periods and is fast gaining a reputation for good diving.
Pulau Sipadan Resort, 1st Floor, Number 484, Block P, Bandar Sabindo, P.O. Box 61120, 91021, Tawau; tel 089–765200/fax 089-763575; e-mail info@lankayan-island.com

and 14:30hrs daily except Fridays, when they are 09:30hrs and 14:30hrs. When I first visited the main feeding station it had too many visitors at feeding times, and the Orangutans and Long-tailed Macaques were snatching visitors' belongings; visitor numbers are now restricted, and the animals no longer give any problem.
Just outside Sandakan, at Mile 7 on Labuk Road, there is a **war memorial** to the hundreds of Australian prisoners of war who died under the Japanese in 1944 on the death marches to Ranau.
Across Sandakan Bay and some 20km (12miles) inland are the **Gomantong Caves**, famous for their bats and swiftlets' nests. The nests, made of saliva, are collected six-monthly for birds'-nest soup. The cave floors are 50cm (20in) or more deep in droppings, so wear sensible footwear.
Further afield is the **Kinabatangan River**, where you can see Proboscis Monkeys and Long-tailed Macaques (Crab-eating Monkeys). These come to the river only at dawn and at dusk, so to catch sight of them you must stay overnight in simple lodges around Sakau and cruise the river in small boats at the appropriate times. You will need fast film if you want to photograph the monkeys.

VISITORS AND TURTLES

On these islands the gravid turtles usually climb the beach between 20:00hrs and dawn, when the tide is high. Visitors are sensibly not allowed to walk around the beach at night, but the rangers carry portable radios and call up the visitors when they find the first turtle laying eggs. Only one turtle may be disturbed each night for photography, and then only once she has laid her eggs. Visitors are afterwards taken to the hatchery, where they can help collect and count the evening's hatchlings and release them into the sea.

PROBLEMS IN PARADISE

Sports divers began venturing into the area in the late 1970s, and a combined WWF/Sabah Parks team made a preliminary marine survey in 1980. Poor anchorage, regular pirate activity and blast-fishing (as late as 1985) kept visitors down, and the few who did venture here used self-contained boats or camped on the beach. By 1988, however, Borneo Divers gained permission to build permanent accommodation, and Mike Wong came on the first of many visits which culminated in his evocative book *Sipadan – Borneo's Underwater Paradise* (1991). In 1989 Jacques Cousteau and his team arrived with the research vessel *Calypso*; the great Frenchman was moved to say: 'I have seen other places like Sipadan, 45 years ago, but now no more. Now we have found an untouched piece of art.'

Since then, the immense popularity of Sipadan diving has produced good and bad results. Several newer diving operators, some of them illegal, tried to squeeze in on the tiny island, while due to the limitations on Sipadan both in size and the type of resort that could be constructed without damaging the environment, some operators built more luxurious resorts on nearby islands. The combined effect was to cause problems both for the environment on land and damage to the reef. Recently, Borneo Divers have set up a recompression chamber on the island and the operators have got together to form Sipadan-Borneo Resort Management in an effort to improve things. Total diver numbers are now restricted to 80.

On the plus side, the turtles and fish on Sipadan have become habituated to the presence of divers, and while local divers already knew it, visiting divers found that although there are not many larger subjects to be found on the other islands, there really were a lot of unusual and colourful small subjects if one searched hard enough in the gloom. This new type of diving was soon called 'muck diving' and is now popular with underwater photographers.

A CORAL PARADISE

Pulau Sipadan's coral, fish and turtle life is prolific: more than 200 species of fish have been recorded and over 70 genera of corals, so that the area matches Australia's Great Barrier Reef in terms of species diversity.

The shallow-water areas are largely covered with corals in excellent condition, with broad expanses of staghorn and table corals, plate and lettuce corals, boulder and brain corals, encrusting corals, bubble corals and solitary mushroom corals. Interspersed among the stony corals are large leathery *Sarcophyton* and *Sinularia* corals, constantly pulsating *Xenia* corals and colourful *Dendronephthya* soft-tree corals. Here, too, are sponges, including vase and barrel sponges, plus sea squirts, oysters and Giant Clams. Although fire coral is uncommon, there are plenty of stinging hydroids.

The drop-off walls are less luxuriant, but have gardens of colourful *Tubastrea* and *Dendrophyllia* species under over-hangs, together with sponges, gorgonian sea fans and *Dendronephthya* soft-tree corals. Deeper down on the walls are huge gorgonian sea fans, black corals, large barrel sponges covered in Alabaster Sea Cucumbers, and very big *Dendronephthya* soft corals.

There was coral and anemone bleaching during the 1997/8 El Niño-Southern Oscillation but both are now recovering.

OUTSTANDING MARINE LIFE

Underwater, Pulau Sipadan has just about everything the Indo-Pacific has to offer. The waters teem with fish, many inquisitive enough to approach divers: expect to be regularly buzzed by shoals of fusiliers, batfish, sweetlips, jacks, goatfish and a huge shoal of Bumphead Parrotfish. At least six species of clownfish inhabit the colourful sea anemones. Timid Whitetip Reef Sharks are common, but the other sharks less so – although Hammerhead, Grey Reef and Variegated (Leopard) Sharks are seen occasionally, as are Manta Rays and Eagle Rays, with Bluespotted Ribbontail Rays being common. If you dive down a shotline in open water off the reef you may encounter tuna.

However, what makes Pulau Sipadan really stand out are the turtles. Massive 140kg (300-pound) Green Turtles and smaller Hawksbill Turtles are everywhere. Often you can see 20–30 on a single dive; usually they ignore you entirely so that they can concentrate on the serious business of eating, sleeping and scratching parasites off their backs on the coral. The main time for nesting is in August. Official egg collectors legally operate here, but nests near

COPING WITH CURRENTS

Pulau Sipadan's currents are unpredictable. On some days Barracuda Point and South Point have ripping currents and on other days they have none. Several times when I've been here there were instances when a three-knot (5.6kph) current pushing us along in one direction would suddenly reverse itself completely. In order not to pass the same points again, we turned around and changed position and/or depth before continuing the dive.

the resorts are often sponsored by tourists to allow the eggs to hatch out. Currently the island is in the care of the Ministry of Tourism and Environmental Development under the Department of Wildlife, which has stationed a team of park rangers on the island to oversee its affairs. The turtles should never be disturbed before they start laying or they will give up and return to the sea, so walking around the island at night without a ranger is forbidden.

Pulau Sipadan can be dived all year round, but the weather is calmest and driest from May to October. August is the local holiday high season. Visibility is unpredictable – it can be murky one day and crystal-clear the next – but in general you can expect it to be about 30m (100ft).

EXCELLENT DIVING

The diving on offer usually consists of three daily boat dives plus unlimited shore dives; if you dive to the limit you should take a day off to de-gas after four or five days. To eliminate anchor damage, the boat dives, from small fibreglass boats holding up to eight divers always accompanied by a resort divemaster, are all drift-dives, even if there is no current. The dive sites are never more than 10min from the resort, so you board the boats from the beach fully kitted up.

On most sites there is excellent diving, whether in deep water on the wall or shallow water on the reef crest. The obvious scheme is to start with the deepest point, gradually rising to shallow water beside or over the reef top, where you can de-gas pleasantly while observing the beauty at this depth. At all sites except Turtle Cavern you can snorkel happily along the edge of the drop-off and see just as much reef life as the divers, although of course you would miss the gorgonian sea fans, black corals and deeper-dwelling sharks and pelagic visitors.

Opposite: *Gorgonian Sea fan (Melithaea squamata).*

Below: *The Coral Trout (Cephalopholis Miniata), one of the most common members of the grouper family.*

Shore dives and night dives are from the beach in front of the chalets, where a swim of 5–10m (16–33ft), depending on the height of the tide, brings you to the drop-off.

Operators will organize guided diving trips to Pulau Kapalai and Pulau Mabul for a fixed fee per boat.

1 THE JETTY, JETTY BEACH AND DROP-OFF BELOW

★★★★★★★★★★★

Location: In front of Borneo Divers and Pulau Sipadan Resort.
Access: Enter the water and swim out 5–10m (16–33ft), depending on the height of the tide.
Conditions: Generally calm; occasionally a slight current.
Average depth: Whatever you like
Maximum depth: 600m (2000ft)

This has to be the world's best beach dive and one of the world's top night dives. The drop-off goes down deeper than divers can dive and of course snorkellers will be limited in their depth, but there is a tremendous amount of interest just in the top 10m (33ft) or so. Under the jetty and to the east of it you find coral with shoals of goatfish and catfish, sea urchins, sea stars and crabs. West of the jetty there is sand frequented by small shoals of fish plus gobies with Bulldozer Shrimps and the occasional large barracuda. (At night I have photographed the rare Zebra Lionfish on this sand.)

Once you go over the drop-off you encounter a huge shoal of jacks and smaller shoals of Spotted Sweetlips and juvenile batfish. Descending the drop-off from 10m to 20m (33–65ft) you come to overhangs and caverns which during the day contain colourful angelfish, butterfly fish, Map and Porcupine Pufferfish, lionfish, scorpionfish and leaf fish, Spotted and Vlaming's Unicornfish, Moorish Idols, Orangestriped and Clown Triggerfish, Giant Moray Eels, various nudibranchs and flat worms, blue and yellow sea squirts, and assorted sponges and anemones (including a rare small white anemone) with clownfish. At night these caves contain parrotfish sleeping in their cocoons, Bumphead Parrotfish, turtles and pufferfish, large *Linckia* sea stars, flashlight fish, scorpionfish, crabs, shrimps and Snowflake Moray Eels. On many night dives here I have been able to study huge sleeping Bumphead Parrotfish and a colossal male Green Turtle at less than arm's-length. Whitetip Reef Sharks patrol the face at dawn and dusk.

2 TURTLE CAVERN

★★★★★

Location: East of the jetty.
Access: Swim out from the jetty beach over the drop-off, turn right (east) and continue along the wall until you reach the cavern entrance on a sandy patch at 18m (60ft).
Conditions: This is an advanced dive on which it is possible to get dangerously lost; the resort operators sensibly insist you are accompanied by one of their divemasters. You require a reliable and powerful underwater light and

> **SIPADAN WILDLIFE**
>
> The attractions of Pulau Sipadan do not begin at the shoreline. On land many bird species have been spotted, including Frigate Birds, Sea Eagles, Reef Egrets, Kingfishers, Wood Pigeons, Nicobar Pigeons, Pied Imperial Pigeons and Sunbirds. It is rumoured that even the weird Megapode has been sighted.
>
> Fruit Bats can be noisy at night. A notorious Monitor Lizard raids the resort's rubbish dump, and the Robber (Coconut) Crab (*Birgus latro*), rare elsewhere, is common here. This crab is diurnal and terrestrial, and has the ability to climb trees. It is prized for its flesh and its edible oil.

a backup. It is easy to stir up silt and spoil the visibility. There may be some current along the wall. Snorkelling is not possible.
Average depth: 15–20m (50–65ft), but the main entrance is at the deepest point
Maximum depth: 21m (70ft)

The famous Turtle Cavern has been romanticized as the place where turtles go to die. The truth is more straightforward. The drowned turtles here probably entered at dusk and got lost in the interconnecting caverns because, when darkness fell, there was no light to guide them out. One of the bodies on view was put here by a film crew.

The caverns were formed as a result of weathering during the last Ice Age when sea levels were 100m (330ft) or so lower than at present. The main entrance is a large cavern on sand at 18m (60ft) with a resident Star Pufferfish and various little shoals of smaller fish. This cavern descends to 21m (70ft). At the back of it you swim up through a tunnel into a smaller cavern which now contains a marlin skeleton (put here by a resort divemaster). The various interconnecting caverns rise to less than 4m (13ft) from the surface and at the furthest point are 70m (230ft) inland from the main entrance. The dark caverns are also home to shoals of flashlight fish and specialized shrimps and crabs.

3 BARRACUDA POINT

★★★★★★★★★★

Location: The northernmost point, on the east side of the reef.
Access: By boat (a few min) east from jetty beach.
Conditions: This dive can be a bit rough, with variable and possibly strong currents that sometimes reverse. Novices should stay with the divemaster.
Average depth: 14m (45ft)
Maximum depth: 600m (2000ft)

This dive got its name from the very large shoal (500–1000) of barracuda often seen on the point. (This shoal is often seen also at the South Point [Site 7] and sometimes disappears for a couple of weeks.) It is interesting to enter the eye of the shoal and experience this immense number of fish circling around you – although some divers freak out when they find so many eyes watching them!

The site varies with depth. In the shallower waters it has coral heads on coral rubble and sand, sloping gently out and down. At the point itself there are Garden Eels; the many Whitetip Reef Sharks that lie on the sand during the day are very timid and difficult to approach closely.

There are few angelfish and butterflyfish here but plenty of just about everything else, including blue and yellow seas quirts, nudibranchs, flat worms, sting rays, moray eels, cuttlefish, many varieties of pufferfish, scorpionfish, stonefish, surgeonfish, flounders and crocodilefish. The area has many large Green Turtles, either sleeping under coral heads while surgeonfish feed on the algae on their shells or scratching themselves on the coral to try to remove barnacles. Trumpetfish hide in whip corals, colourful feather stars spread out in the current on any support they can find, and various pelagic species cruise around.

4 CORAL GARDENS

★★★★★★★★★★★

Location: The northeast face of the reef, southeast of Barracuda Point.
Access: By boat (5min) east and then south around the island from the jetty beach.
Conditions: Normally a gentle current; occasionally stronger.
Average depth: 10m (33ft) along the reef crest
Maximum depth: 600m (2000ft)
You can descend the drop-off, but the beauty of this dive is to be found on the coral crest. Vast fields of stony corals are interspersed with smaller areas of soft corals, large boulder corals and large leathery corals and sponges. The staghorn corals are particularly prolific and colourful. This is a paradise for photographers, with just about every type of colourful Pacific reef fish you could think of, from tiny Anthias, Fire Gobies, Chromis, sergeant majors and damselfish through most of the smaller angelfish and butterflyfish to the larger Emperor, Yellowmask and Six-band angelfish. There are shoals of jacks, Rainbow Runners, fusiliers, goatfish and snappers. On one dive here I encountered a shoal of nearly 100 Bumphead Parrotfish. Batfish hover at cleaning stations, and Powder-blue Surgeonfish, Sleek, Spotted and Vlaming's Unicornfish, Picasso, Orangestriped, Titan and Clown Triggerfish, Moorish Idols and bannerfish all flit among the corals. Groupers, Coral Trout, hawkfish, soldierfish, Golden Rabbitfish, squirrelfish and bigeyes pause on or under corals. Parrotfish and Giant Wrasse cruise around, and a remarkable variety of anemones play host

to clownfish. Colourful feather stars are everywhere.

As well as the more common Green Turtles, Hawksbill Turtles can be found on the edge of the drop-off, often feeding on sponges.

5 WHITETIP AVENUE AND MID REEF

★★★★★★★★★★★

Location: The central part of the east face of the reef.
Access: By boat (10min) east and then south around the island from the jetty beach.
Conditions: Current usually gentle; can get stronger. Suitable for inexperienced divers *except* deep over the drop-off.
Average depth: 16m (52ft) for the reef crest
Maximum depth: 600m (2000ft)
There are two dives here, either on the reef crest or over the drop-off in deeper water. The reef crest is covered in stony and soft corals with most of the colourful Pacific reef fish you associate with them as well as oysters, Giant Clams and many turtles.

In deeper water over the drop-off, especially between 30m (100ft) and 50m (165ft), there are big black corals, huge gorgonian sea fans (often hiding Longnose Hawkfish and adorned with feather stars) and many large barrel sponges covered in Alabaster Sea Cucumbers. In strong currents *Dendronephthya* soft tree corals swell up to impressive dimensions. Further down, Whitetip Reef Sharks and Grey Reef Sharks cruise the wall. In strong currents, I have started a dive at Mid Reef or Turtle Patch (Site 6) and finished at the jetty beach, having in the interim used up the 36-exposure films in both my cameras!

6 TURTLE PATCH

★★★★★★★★★★★

Location: The southern end of the east face of the reef.
Access: By boat (10min) east and then south around the island from the jetty beach.
Conditions: Usually calm with a light current, but the current can get stronger.
Average depth: 14m (45ft)
Maximum depth: 600m (2000ft)
This dive is very similar to Mid Reef and Whitetip Avenue (Site 5) but with even more turtles. I once spent 20min here photographing a Hawksbill Turtle close-up while it ripped apart a sponge deep in a crevice between corals; it was too intent on feeding to pay any attention to me! This is another area where I have encountered the huge shoal of Bumphead Parrotfish mentioned at Site 4. Immature Whitetip Reef Sharks can be found hiding in small coral crevices. There are lots of very large table corals.

7 **SOUTH POINT**

8 **STAGHORN CREST**

9 **LOBSTER LAIRS**

★★★★★★★★★★

Location: The southern end of the reef: the South Point is the southernmost point of the east face; Staghorn Crest is immediately west of South Point; Lobster Lairs is at the southern end of the west face.

Access: By boat (10min) either way around the island from the jetty beach.

Conditions: Like Barracuda Point (Site 3) these dives can be a bit rough, with variable and often strong currents which may reverse during the dive. Novices should stay with the divemaster.

Average depth: 20m (65ft)

Maximum depth: 600m (2000ft)

In many ways these dives are rather similar to Barracuda Point (Site 3), with coral heads on coral rubble and sand. The currents are often too strong for the less sturdy corals and their associated fish, but just about everything else is to be found here.

Bracing yourself for photography can be difficult, but there is plenty worth photographing. The huge Barracuda shoal (see Site 3) is often seen on the South Point, as are other pelagic species including Manta Rays and Eagle Rays. A dozen or more Whitetip Reef Sharks and the occasional Leopard (Variegated) Shark rest on the sand at the point. There are lots of shoaling fish, especially fusiliers, snappers and Rainbow Runners, plus unicornfish, batfish, surgeonfish, jacks, scorpionfish, stonefish, crocodilefish, flounders, moray eels, pufferfish, feather stars and the inevitable turtles – large lone Green Turtles sleeping or scratching themselves and Hawksbill Turtles feeding. There are some big blast-fishing craters around the South Point and Staghorn Crest, and lots of broken coral at Lobster Lairs. Also at Lobster Lairs are several narrow crevices in the coral where lobsters hide. The reef slopes gently out and down, but there is not much of interest below 30m (100ft).

10 **HANGING GARDENS**

11 **WEST RIDGE**

12 **NORTH POINT**

★★★★★★★★★★

Location: The west face of the reef: Hanging Gardens is west–southwest of the navigation light tower; West Ridge is west of the island itself; North Point is the northernmost point of the west face.

Access: By boat (5min) west and then south around the island from the jetty beach.

Conditions: Usually some current, often enough to push you all the way back to the jetty beach. Snorkelling is possible but not under the overhangs in deep water.

Average depth: 18m (60ft)

Maximum depth: 600m (2000ft)

You swim above a shallow coral-covered reef crest, then over the drop-off and down the wall, which has lots of overhangs containing *Tubastrea* and *Dendrophyllia* corals, large gorgonian sea fans (hiding Longnose Hawkfish), black corals, sponges and barrel sponges – hence the name 'Hanging Gardens'. There are also plenty of nudibranchs, flat worms and feather stars.

The reef crest covering consists of hard and soft corals with all varieties of Pacific reef fish including lionfish, scorpionfish, stonefish, pufferfish, batfish, rabbitfish, barracuda and moray eels. There are also shoals of jacks, sweetlips, snappers, fusiliers, Rainbow Runners and goatfish, plus many species of sea anemones and clownfish.

Above: *The tiny Long-nosed Hawkfish (Oxycirrhites typus) less than 5cm (2in). It is seen here camouflaged on a gorgonian sea fan.*

Below: *During the day the Goggle Eye or Big Eye (Priacanthus hamrur) can be found hanging under reefs or in caves. It feeds at night.*

Pulau Mabul

Situated within easy diving-boat distance of Pulau Sipadan, the diving resorts on Pulau Mabul and Pulau Kapalai were originally developed as a way of having more luxurious accommodation than could be constructed on Pulau Sipadan for ecological reasons together with overcrowding and the risk that Pulau Sipadan could become Indonesian territory. However, divers making dives locally late in the day or at night soon realized that there was good muck diving (see page 124) so these sites have become diving destinations in their own right.

PULAU MABUL

A small sandy island slightly larger than Pulau Sipadan with coconut palms, a police post and a semi-legal fishing village of Filipino Sea Gypsies on its northwestern beach, Pulau Mabul lies on the northern end of a larger reef on the edge of the continental shelf.

The diving is mainly sand and coral rubble covered in algae and the visibility can be as low as 3m (10ft) but every hole seems to be inhabited: Ghost Pipefish, frogfish, gobies, shrimps, Mandarinfish, Crocodilefish, Flamboyant Cuttlefish, cowfish and numerous species of nudibranchs. Sea snakes are not commonly seen underwater, but they can sometimes be found on land at night.

The most popular dives are described clockwise from the SMART jetty (Explore Asia Tours, formally known as Sipadan-Mabul Regal Tours).

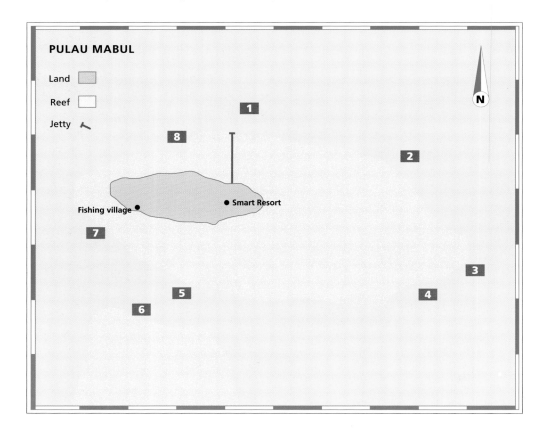

PULAU MABUL

Land
Reef
Jetty

N

1
8
2
Fishing village
Smart Resort
7
3
5
4
6

1 FROGGY LAIR

★★★★★★

Location: From the SMART jetty to the outer huts of Siapadan Water Village.
Access: From shore or by boat.
Conditions: Calm
Average depth: 10m (35ft)
Maximum depth: 15m (45ft)
Visibility: 3m (10ft)
Among the detritus and coral smothered by silt on a 45-degree slope is a veritable smorgasbord of well-camouflaged creatures: Crocodile fish, frogfish, Flying gurnards, Pipefish, Ghost Pipefish, eels, Leaf Fish, Scorpionfish, Stonefish, Seahorses, Mandarinfish, Mantis Shrimps, sea urchins and nudibranchs.

2 CORAL REEF GARDENS

★★★★★★

Location: Southeast side of the reef.
Access: By boat.
Conditions: Calm
Average depth: 5m (15ft)
Maximum depth: 15m (50ft)
Visibility: 3m (10ft)
This site is not among the most popular for muck diving as it is one of the better sites on Mabul for diver training. There are soft corals and anemones while the fish life includes angelfish, butterflyfish, batfish, lionfish, scorpionfish, jacks and fusiliers.

3 EEL GARDEN

★★★★★★

Location: The southeast end of the reef.
Access: By boat.
Conditions: Calm
Average depth: 18m (60ft)
Maximum depth: 20m (65ft)
Visibility: 3m (10ft)
Eel Garden is named after its many eels, including the Blue Ribbon Eel. Although it drops into deeper water, this site would be much the same as Pulau Sipadan except for the poor visibility so the main dive is in shallow water. Small coral mounds on a sandy flat with gobies accompanied by their symbiotic shrimps, the area also has Mantis Shrimps, sea stars, anemones with clownfish and nudibranchs.

Despite the gloom there are the more common reef inhabitants on display from gorgonians to angelfish, butterflyfish, batfish, lionfish and even Bumphead Parrotfish.

4 RAY POINT

★★★★★★★★

Location: The southwest side of the reef.
Access: By boat.
Conditions: Calm, but often with some current.
Average depth: 10m (35ft)
Maximum depth: 1.5m (5ft)
Visibility: 5m (15ft)
A steeper slope descending deeper in a succession of terraces and often slightly better visibility due to the current, which also produces much healthier corals and gorgonians.

The fish life is more like that of Pulau Sipadan, great variety including groupers, snappers, Bigeye Trevallies, angelfish, butterflyfish, triggerfish, rabbitfish, moray eels, Crocodilefish, lionfish, scorpionfish, stonefish and the reason for the name, Bluespotted Ribbontail Rays.

5 LOBSTER WALL

★★★★★★★★

Location: The west side of the reef.
Access: By boat.
Conditions: Calm, but often with some current.
Average depth: 40m (130ft)
Maximum depth: 150m (465ft+)
Visibility: 10m (35ft)
A deeper dive on what passes for a wall with a cave containing lobsters. The visibility is better because of the current and the sediment can fall away so again there is plenty to see here: moray eels, groupers, Bigeye Trevallies, clownfish in anemones, Ghost Pipefish, Seahorses, pufferfish, angelfish, butterflyfish, triggerfish, rabbitfish, Crocodilefish, lionfish, scorpionfish and stonefish.

6 NUDIBRANCH CENTRE

★★★★★★★★

Location: Northwest of Lobster Wall (site 5).
Access: By boat.
Conditions: Calm, but often with some current.
Average depth: 20m (65ft)
Maximum depth: 150m+ (465ft+)

Visibility: 10m (35ft)

Mostly treated as a shallow dive, Nudibranch Centre has a profusion of nudibranchs among a myriad of reef fish: shoals of catfish, moray eels, groupers, clownfish in anemones, Parrotfish, Mandarinfish, gobies, jawfish, Pipefish, Seahorses, pufferfish, angelfish, butterflyfish, triggerfish, rabbitfish, Crocodilefish, lionfish, scorpionfish and stonefish.

7 PANGLIMA REEF

★★★★★★

Location: West of the fishing village on the west beach.
Access: By boat.
Conditions: Calm
Average depth: 5m (15ft)
Maximum depth: 20m (65ft)
Visibility: 3m (10ft)

Panglima Reef has a profusion of nudibranchs among soft corals, pipefish, Crocodilefish, cuttlefish, shoals of catfish, moray eels, groupers, clownfish in anemones, parrotfish, Mandarinfish, gobies, jawfish, pipefish, Seahorses, puffer-

fish, angelfish, butterflyfish, triggerfish, rabbitfish, Crocodilefish, lionfish, scorpionfish and stonefish.

8 CROCODILE AVENUE

Location: Northwest of the SMART jetty.
Access: By boat.
Conditions: Calm
Average depth: 7m (25ft)
Maximum depth: 15m (50ft)
Visibility: 3m (10ft)

This dive could be a definition for muck di ving, at first it looks completely lifeless but on detailed inspection it is found to be full of juveniles and other small creatures.

From 2–15m (6½–50ft) on a 45-degree slope there are Crocodilefish, Leaf Fish, Seahorses, pipefish, frogfish, Mandarinfish, gurnards, soles, snake eels, catfish, juvenile cuttlefish, Ghost Pipefish, lionfish, scorpionfish, gobies, blennies and Flamboyant Cuttlefish. At night there are squid.

Pulau Kapalai

Only 15 minutes from Pulau Sipadan, between Pulau Sipadan and Pulau Mabul, Pulau Kapalai has been a macro-photography destination for local divers in the know for many years, Danny Chin and Captain Sim mentioned it to me in the early 1990s. Once an island it has slowly eroded away so that nowadays only a sandbar is visible at low tide. The diving resort is the upmarket equivalent of a Malay or Filipino Sea Gypsy water village, all structures being built above the sea on stilts.

As with Pulau Mabul, knowledgeable dive masters lead you around some of the best muck diving in the world, Flamboyant Cuttlefish, Blue-ringed Octopus, dragonets, mating Mandarinfish, frogfish, ribbon eels, jawfish and Harlequin Ghost Pipefish are seen on a regular basis. The colourful Mandarinfish and the Flamboyant Cuttlefish with colours flashing along its body are memorable sights.

A weak current produces better visibility and there are 18 recognized dive sites though the species found are common to most of them if you look hard enough, I have only listed three here.

1 MANDARIN VALLEY

★★★★★★★★

Location: The Sipadan–Kapalai resort's jetty on the north side of the reef.

Access: From shore or by boat.
Conditions: Calm
Average depth: 8m (25ft)
Maximum depth: 20m (65ft)
Visibility: 8m (25ft)

There is plenty of healthy coral here and many anemones and sponges, even Bumphead Parrot fish are seen occasionally. Mandarinfish, Ghost Pipefish, frog-fish, octopuses, common cuttlefish, Flamboyant Cuttlefish, nudibranchs, gobies, cardinalfish, stonefish, Crocodilefish, Moorish Idols, leaf fish, scorpionfish, lion-fish, jawfish, sea urchins, sea stars, sea cucumbers and feather stars are among the creatures found.

2 GURNARD GROUND

★★★★★★★★★

Location: North of the northeast point of the reef.
Access: By boat.
Conditions: Calm
Average depth: 9m (30ft)
Maximum depth: 20m (65ft)
Visibility: 8m (25ft)
This dive site is similar to Mandarin Valley but without the Mandarinfish. Look hard and there are plenty of camouflaged creatures to find. Stonefish stay still, imitating rocks covered in sand or algae, Ghost Pipefish and leaf fish wave about in the current, imitating leaves, Seahorses hide and frogfish have the colour of the nearest sponges.

Ribbon Eels, moray eels, Ghost Pipefish, frogfish,

octopuses, common cuttlefish, nudibranchs, flatworms, gobies, blennies, cardinalfish, stonefish, Crocodilefish, Moorish Idols, angelfish, butterflyfish, Humphead (Napoleon) Wrasse can also be spotted.

3 STINGRAY CITY

★★★★★★★★★

Location: On the west side of the reef.
Access: By boat.
Conditions: Calm
Average depth: 9m (30ft)
Maximum depth: 13m (45ft)
Visibility: 8m (25ft)
Also called Spotted Ray Channel, the name of this rich site comes from the Bluespotted Ribbontail Rays com-mon here. Stony and soft corals, gorgonians, Ribbon Eels, moray eels, Ghost Pipefish, frogfish, octopuses, common cuttlefish, nudibranchs, flatworms, gobies, blennies, cardinalfish, stonefish, Crocodilefish, Moorish Idols, angelfish, butterflyfish, Humphead (Napoleon) Wrasse, leaf fish, scorpionfish, lionfish, dragonets, gurnards, sea urchins, sea stars, sea cucumbers and feather stars, shrimps and juvenile lobsters are common.

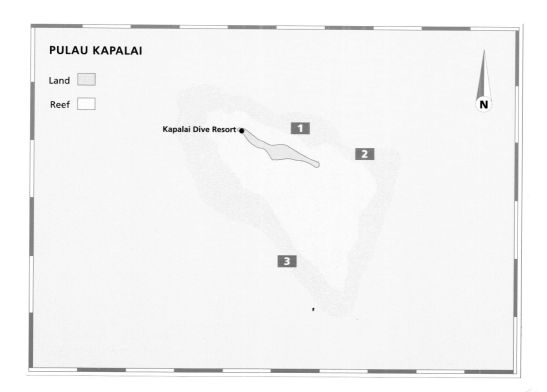

How to Get There

Kota Kinabalu is easily accessible by international flights from Kuala Lumpur, Hong Kong, Manila, Singapore, Bangkok, Brunei, Taipei and Seoul. From Kota Kinabalu you take a short flight by Malaysian Airlines Boeing 737 to Tawau. You can also book seats on a STOL aircraft flight which flies once a week from Kota Kinabalu to Semporna direct.

From Tawau you transfer by road to the jetty by the Dragon Inn in Semporna. This can take 1–2hr depending on the vehicle and the driver. From Semporna it is 45min by speedboat to Pulau Sipadan. This crossing can be bumpy, so make sure that fragile equipment is suitably packed.

Wealthy clients can now take a helicopter direct from Tawau Airport to the resorts on Pulau Sipadan.

Helicopter Services

For details of the services available, refer to the directory section covering Turtle Islands Park (page 126).

Where to Stay

Most divers will arrive as part of a package trip and would normally stay overnight in Kota Kinabalu before taking an early-morning flight to Tawau, then travelling on to Semporna and Pulau Sipadan.

If you wish to stay in Semporna there is the Dragon Inn, near the departure jetty for Pulau Sipadan. Constructed of wood and built on stilts above the water, it is similar to the houses in the nearby Bajau water villages. It has its own restaurant but you would be wise to avoid the lobsters, kept in cages below the hotel in water which contains much of the village's effluent.

Dragon Inn Hotel Jalan Tastan, PO Box 6 91307 Semporna; tel 089–781088/fax 089–781559

The cheaper hotels in Tawau are best avoided. The most commonly used is:

Hotel Emas Jalan Utara. Postal Address: PO Box 569, New North Road, 91007 Tawau; tel 089–762000/fax 089–763569

Others include (both in the upper price range):

Belmont Marco Polo Hotel
Jalan Clinic, PO Box 1003, 91007 Tawau; tel 089–777988/fax 089–763739

Hotel Merdeka P.O. Box 60276, Jalan Masjid, 91007 Tawau; tel 089–776655/fax 089–761743

For details of the accommodation offered by the dive operators, see below.

Where to Eat

The hotels have their own westernized restaurants. If you are looking for fast food, turn right out of the main entrance of hotel Emas and right again; on the next corner there is a Kentucky Fried Chicken-type restaurant. If, on the other hand, you are looking for a top-quality Western-style restaurant I can recommend

XO Steakhouse Ground Floor, TB 330B, Block 42, Fajar Complex, Tawau; tel 089–764186

Dive Facilities

The resort operators on Pulau Sipadan itself are required by law to use water-desalination plants for fresh water and to ensure that sewage and rubbish do not find their way into the sea.

Borneo Divers (address below), the original and the largest Pulau Sipadan operator, has the prime position along the beach either side of the jetty, with easy access across the beach to the drop-off. The company is very strong in the US, European and Australian markets, and prefers to deal through agents in the country of sale. These agents handle flights from the country of origin to Kota Kinabalu, where Borneo Divers takes over, handling accommodation, transfers and any side tours within Malaysia or Indonesia (Sangalaki). Refer to pages 140–141 for more about Borneo Divers and a list of the company's overseas agents.

Borneo Divers have several female divemasters, which some novices, ladies and families may feel more comfortable with.

The smaller **Pulau Sipadan Resort** also caters for deep-sea fishing and local non-diving tourists, and has more of a local atmosphere. It is situated along the beach west of and adjacent to Borneo Divers, also having easy access across the beach to the drop-off.

Pulau Sipadan Resort deals in direct bookings as well as agency bookings. It is popular with local and expatriate divers from Brunei, Malaysia and Singapore. Contact Veronica Lee by fax, post or telephone (see details below) and she will handle all accommodation and transfers from Kota Kinabalu.

The other operators are spread around the island, further away from the jetty and the drop-off.

Dive-shops

The dive operators have small shops on the island selling batteries, print film, toiletries and other sundry items. Basic diving and snorkelling equipment is available for hire. Borneo Divers also have a dive-shop at their Tawau office:

Borneo Divers, TB 46 Jalan Dunlop, Tawau; tel 089–761259/fax 089–761691

Diver Training
Sipadan-Borneo Resort Management Sdn. Bhd., tel 088–242407/fax 088–242417; e-mail sbrm@tm.net.my

Abdillah Sipadan Paradise, Adventure Journey World Travel (Borneo) Sdn. Bhd., P.O. Box 12248, Ground Floor, Lot 5, Block A, Taman Fortuna Shoplots, Jalan Panampang, 88825 Kota Kinabalu; tel 088–221586/fax 088–248331; e-mail jworld@po.jaring.my; www.borneo.org/asp. PADI dive guides.

Borneo Divers and Sea Sports (Sabah) Sdn. Bhd., Locked Bag 194, 9th Floor, Menara Jubili, 53 Jalan Gaya, 88000 Kota Kinabalu; tel 088–222226/fax 088–221550; e-mail bdivers@po.jaring.my; www.jaring.my/bdivers. Borneo Divers started the first dive training facility in Borneo, the first PADI Dive Centre, PADI 5-star Dive Centre, PADI 5-star Instructor Development Centre and now the first PADI 5-star Career Development Centre.

Pulau Sipadan Resort & Tours Sdn. Bhd., 1st Floor, Number 484, Block P, Bandar Sabindo, P.O. Box 61120, 91021 Tawau; tel 089–765200/fax 089–763575; e-mail psrt@po.jaring.my; www.sipadan-resort.com. PADI Training.

Sipadan Dive Centre Sdn. Bhd., A1103, 11th Floor, Wisma Merdeka, Jalan Tun Razak, 88000 Kota Kinabalu; tel 088–240584/fax 088–240415; e-mail sipadan@po.jaring.my; www.jaring.my/sipadan. PADI 5-star Dive Centre.

Sipadan Lodge, Borneo Sea Adventures Sdn. Bhd., 1st Floor, 8A Karamunsing Warehouse, P.O.Box 10134, Kota Kinabalu; tel 088–230000/fax 088–221106; e-mail bornsea@pop1.jaring.my; www.sipadanlodge.com.my. PADI dive guides.

Pulau Mabul
Explore Asia Tours Sdn. Bhd. (formerly known as Sipadan-Mabul Regal Tours [SMART]), P.O.Box 15571, 88864 Kota Kinabalu; tel 088–230006/fax 088–242003; e-mail mabul@po.jaring.my; www.sipadan-mabul.com.my. PADI training, TDI and PADI Basic Nitrox and ScubaZoo Images, video & E6 processing facility; tel 088–232068/fax 088–237068; e-mail info@scubazoo.com; www.scubazoo.com.

Seaventures Tours & Travel Sdn. Bhd., 4th Floor, Rooms 422-424, Wisma Sabah, 88300 Kota Kinabalu; tel 088–261669/fax 088–251667; e-mail seavent@po.jaring.my; www.borneo-online.com.my/sv. PADI diving courses up to Assistant Instructor.

Sipadan Water Village Resort Sdn. Bhd., P.O. Box 62156, TB 226, Lot 3, 1st Floor, Wisma MAA, Town Ext. II, 91031 Tawau; tel 089–752996/fax 089–752997; e-mail sww@sipadan-village.com.my; www.sipadan-village.com.my. CMAS and PADI courses up Divemaster; ScubaZoo Images, video & E6 processing facility.

Pulau Kapalai
Sipadan-Kapalai Dive Resort
(see address for Pulau Sipadan Resort); e-mail kapalai@tm.net.my. PADI training.
Pandanan and Mataking
Pasir Pandanan-Semporna Island Resort, Tanjung Aru Tours & Travel, Kota Kinabalu; tel 088–256676/fax 088–240966. PADI dive guides.

Roach Reefs Resort
Roach Reefs Resort Sdn. Bhd., 52, Dunlop Street, P.O. Box 306, 91007 Tawau; tel 089-763060/fax 089-773066
General Sales Agent: North Borneo Dive & Sea Sports Sdn. Bhd., TB:534, Hotel Grace Inn, G/F, Jalan Haji Karim, Tacoln Complex, 91000 Tawau; tel 089-769950/fax 089-768531; e-mail borneo_tours@hotmail.com; www.fortunecity.com/marina/fantasy/132/rrr. htm. PADI courses up to Assistant Instructor.

Leisure Divers Sdn. Bhd., Lot No 25-UG-13 Plaza Prima, Old Klang Road 58200, Kuala Lumpur; tel/fax 03-7826059; e-mail jeffdive@ tm.net.my; http://members.xoom.com/ leisurediver. SSI Open Water & Advanced Scuba Diving Courses.

All islands accessed from Semporna
North Borneo Dive & Sea Sports also run day trips to almost all of the islands from the Dragon Inn Hotel in Semporna. (See address above)

Cheap accommodation on many of the islands including Mabul Backpackers Lodge and Darval Bay, Semporna:
Setarawarni Tourism Sdn. Bhd., Ground floor Seafest Inn, Jalan Kastam, Semporna; tel/fax 089-782366; e-mail setarawarni@ hotmail.com

FILM PROCESSING

ScubaZoo have E6 processing at Explore Asia Tours Sdn. Bhd. (formally known as Sipadan-Mabul Regal Tours [SMART]) and Siapadan Water Village on Pulau Mabul, and there are larger commercial processors at Sandakan and Kota Kinabalu; refer to the directories covering

Turtle Islands Park (page 122) and Tunku Abdul Rahman Marine Park (page 102).

ScubaZoo Images, PO Box 20149, Pejabat Pos Luyang, 88758 Kota Kinabalu, Sabah; tel 088-232068/fax 088-237068; email Info@scubazoo.com; www.scubazoo.com

HOSPITALS

Tawau General Hospital
PO Box 67, 91007 Tawau; tel 089–763533

Semporna District Hospital PO Box 80 91307, Semporna; tel 089–781522

LOCAL HIGHLIGHTS

Nearby are the islands of the proposed Semporna Marine Park (see page 128), but these are of little interest by comparison with Pulau Sipadan itself.

Semporna has a busy market and Bajau water villages. The Semporna Ocean Tourism Centre is worth a visit if only to admire its location on stilts atop a causeway; its aquarium is best left unmentioned. From Semporna you can take day-trips to the beaches of Pulau Gaya, Pulau Mabul and Pulau Sibuon.

The people in the 'Icebox' **Bajau water village** in Tawau are very friendly. You can organize a day visit to the local **cocoa estates** through Hotel Emas (see address above).

If you are energetic, try a few days' trekking along the jungle trails of the **Danum Valley Field Centre**. Accommodation is limited (I had to camp), so organize this – and transport – in advance. Bookings are through Innprise Corporation Sdn Bhd, Sadong Jaya, Kota Kinabalu (tel 088–243245), which also has a regional office in Lahad Datu (tel

KINABANTANGAN RIVER AND GOMANTONG CAVES

Nature enthusiasts will enjoy a trip on the **Kinabantangan River**. Here in Lower Kinabantangan, you can see the strange-looking proboscis monkeys with their big protruding noses. The species is known as *Orang Belanda* or 'Dutchman', named after early Dutch missionaries whose European noses seemed large to the local people. These monkeys can be seen crashing from tree to tree by the water. Orangutans and elephants also inhabit this area but are rarely to be seen. Between the road to the village of Sukau and the Kinabantangan River lie the **Gomantong Caves**, home to millions of bats and swiftlets whose nests are much prized by the Chinese for birds' nest soup.

089–81092).

If you have the time to go by road from Semporna to Sandakan, then as well as Danum Valley you can visit **Batuh Peteh Tulug Burial Caves** and the **Gomantong Caves**, and take a look at the Proboscis Monkeys on the **Kinabatangan River**.

Don't miss the **Sepilok Orangutan Rehabilitation Centre**.

A tranquil scene at Borneo Divers' resort on Pulau Sipadan which can be dived all year round.

Randy Davis and Ron Holland, two expatriate divers who worked professionally in Sabah, Labuan and Sarawak, as well as diving for pleasure, found themselves regularly being asked to train others. In 1983 they got together with Clement Lee and Samson Shak to set up Borneo Divers. The company opened for business in 1984 and was incorporated under Malaysian Law on 10 August. It operated from a small dive-shop beside the Tanjung Aru Resort, outside Kota Kinabalu.

RAPID EXPANSION

After initial hiccups the business rapidly expanded in the fields of both commercial and recreational diving. Borneo Divers started taking trips to Pulau Sipadan in 1985, sleeping in tents; the company built its first dive-lodge there in 1989. In 1991 Clement Lee became Malaysia's first PADI course director, the highest level of teaching within PADI.

In 1992 the company transferred its jointly owned commercial section, Borneo Subsea Services (Malaysia) Sdn Bhd, to the Asia Supply Base at Labuan, also opening another recreational centre and dive-shop there. In 1993 it opened P.T. Sangalaki Dive Resort.

The subsidiary company, Borneo Divers And Sea Sports (KL) Sdn. Bhd. in Petaling Jaya was incorporated in July 1994. Under director-in-charge, professional underwater photographer Daniel D'Orville, the Kuala Lumpur branch oversees Borneo Divers and Sea Sports services and operation throughout Peninsula Malaysia, Singapore and Thailand and organises the Annual Borneo Underwater Photo-Shoot-out. As well as offering PADI training courses, the Underwater Photography department stocks most popular underwater cameras and housings.

A THRIVING DIVE COMPANY

Today Borneo Divers is the largest professional full-service dive company in Southeast Asia. The original four directors remain in office and still dive regularly, a fact that may have no small influence on the company's commercial success. Clement Lee Ngak Yeo, one of the first two Malaysian PADI Course Directors, is now Managing Director. Randy Davis looks after the many Labuan Sport and commercial facilities including commercial diving, underwater salvage operations, technical diving and the subsidiary company Borneo Yacht & Marine Services (Labuan) Sdn. Bhd. Ron Holland covers Borneo Divers (Sabah), Sangalaki Island Dive Resort and research and development. Samson Shak is the director in-charge for Borneo Divers Sipadan Island Dive Lodge and Daniel D'Orville oversees the overall company marketing and administration for Borneo Divers' subsidiary – Borneo Divers and Sea Sports (Kuala Lumpur) Sdn. Bhd.

The company's Commercial operations based at Labuan are ideally situated for rapid transport to the offshore oilfields industry as well as for local underwater inspection and surveys with capabilities for diving on air to 50m (165ft), mixed gas facilities, Remotely Operated Vehicles (ROVs) and yacht work.

ENVIRONMENTALLY FRIENDLY

Borneo Divers has always been at the forefront of conservation, both on land and underwater. Clients are not allowed to spear fish or collect marine animals, dead or alive. The company has sponsored numerous underwater and beach clean-ups as well as Crown-of-Thorns Starfish harvests from threatened areas in Tunku Abdul Rahman Park. It actively promotes PADI's project AWARE – Aquatic World Awareness Responsibility Education – which is a 10-year programme to educate new divers and re-educate existing divers about taking care of, and cleaning up, the marine environment. It has co-sponsored several WWF–University of Malaysia environmental studies on Pulau Sipadan, where it was the first to instal a water-desalination plant and use biodegradable soaps and other items. It is implementing the same policies at P.T. Sangalaki Dive Resort.

AGENTS

Borneo Divers have agents all over the world. The contact details opposite are only a selection. If you need further details contact the main office at the following address:

Borneo Divers and Sea Sports (Sabah) Sdn. Bhd., Locked Bag 194, 9th Floor, Menara Jubili, 53 Jalan Gaya, 88000 Kota Kinabalu; tel 088-222226/fax 088-221550; e-mail bdivers@po.jaring.my; www.jaring.my/bdivers

AGENTS

AUSTRALIA
Dive Adventures, Level 9, 32 York Street, Sydney, New South Wales, 2000 Australia tel 02-92994633/fax 02-92994644. Melbourne: tel 03-95342700/fax 03-95342055; e-mail adventure@magna.com.au

AUSTRIA
Diving Sports & Travel, Schonbrunner Strabe 68, A-1050 Wien, Austria; tel 01-5452040/fax 01-5452041

CANADA
Squba Holidays, 105 Wharncliffe Road, South London, Ontario, N6J 2K2 Canada; tel 519-6611095/fax 519-6610144; e-mail squba@sympatico.ca

DENMARK
Atlantis Rejser, NY Vestergade 9, 1471 KBH.K, Denmark; tel 33324840/fax 33324842; e-mail atlantis@rejser.ithouse.dk

FRANCE
Blue Lagoon Voyages, 26 Rue De Maubeuge, 75009 Paris, France; tel 01-42829540/fax 01-40230143

GERMANY
Air Aqua Reisen GMBH, Ruttenscheider Street 14, 45128 Essen; tel 0201-790079/fax 0201-780750

Martin Moxter Tauchreisen, An Der Theisenmuhle 1, 633303 Dreieich, Germany; tel 06103 65492/fax 06103 64891; e-mail mmox@aol.com

Schoner Tauchen, Uwe Nehls, Alter Postweg 97, 28207 Bremen; tel 0421-450010/fax 0421-450080

HOLLAND
Sport Reizen Service, Nijverheidsweg 14, NL-4731 CZ, Cudenbosch, Holland; tel 0165-313463/fax 0165-318493; e-mail sportreizen@wxs.nl

ITALY
Aquadiving Tours, Piazzale Innocenti, 12/13 61100, Pesaro Italy; tel 0721-65770/fax 0721-65376; e-mail aquadiving@netco.it

SWITZERLAND
Intens Travel AG, Dorfplatz 6, 6330 Cham, Switzerland; tel 041-7803366/fax 041-4178090; e-mail intens.travel@intens.ch

UNITED KINGDOM
Hayes and Jarvis (Travel) Ltd, Hayes House, 152 King Street, London W6 0QU; tel 020-87480088/fax 020-87410299; e-mail diving@hayes-jarvis.com

Jebsens Travel Ltd, Jebsen House, 16-18 Denbigh Street, SW1V 2ER London; tel 020-79320998/fax 020-78217232 e-mail scuba@jebsons.co.uk

USA
Adventure Express Travel, 650 Fifth Street, Suite 505, CA 94107, San Francisco, United States of America; tel 800-4430799/fax 415-4420289; e-mail adventure @adventureexpress.com

Island Dreams Travel, 8582 Katy Freeway, Suite 118, Houston, 77024 Texas, United States of America; tel 800-3466116/fax 713-9738585; e-mail info@islandream.com

Reef & Rainforest Worldwide Adventure Travel, 4000 Bridgeway, Suite #103, Sausalito, CA 94965-1444, United States of America; tel 800-7949767/fax 206-415-2891763; e-mail rnrtravel@aol.com

Tropical Adventure, 111 Second North, Seattle 98109, Washington, United States of America; tel 800-7234530/fax 206-4415431; e-mail dive@divetropical.com

Pulau Sipadan must have the best and easiest shore diving in the world. The drop-off is only a few metres from your accommodation.

SANGALAKI (DIVING'S NEW FRONTIER)

Sangalaki is in fact in Indonesia, but I have included it here because it is most easily accessible from Malaysian Borneo.

Once the company had completed its dive resort on Pulau Sipadan (see page 130), Borneo Divers began reconnoitring for good diving among the islands and reefs south of that island. Local fishermen told the company of an island, Pulau Kakaban, which had a lake containing millions of jellyfish. Pulau Kakaban was found indeed to offer good diving, but its surrounding mangrove swamps made it unsuitable for resort development. However, the nearby island of Pulau Sangalaki also had good diving and was similar to Pulau Sipadan, 190km (120 miles) to the north, so it was decided to develop Pulau Sangalaki Resort.

A TROPICAL PARADISE

About 12ha (30 acres) in area, the island is covered in dense tropical forest surrounded by white, sandy beaches that are perfect for turtles laying eggs. You can walk right round it in 20min. The tidal range is 2.5m (8ft) and the reefs extend some 600–1000m (660–1100yd) out, continuing as gentle slopes. A small boat channel has been cut through the outer reef. All the dive sites around Pulau Sangalaki are 10–15min from the resort by fast speedboat. Most of the diving is drift-diving. You can snorkel from the boat, particularly among the Manta Rays, which are very approachable. When the tide is in you can board the dive boat at the beach, but by the time you return the boat will ground some 150m (500ft) out, leaving you to walk the rest of the way. Similarly, you will have to walk out to the boat for the next dive, but by the time you return the tide will allow the boat right up to the main beach again. This walking is no particular hardship, as there are plenty of willing Borneo Divers staff to carry your equipment.

PULAU KAKABAN, DERAWAN, MARATUA AND MUARES REEFS

Some 25min away by boat is Pulau Kakaban, where there are walls to 240m (800ft) with lots of pelagic species. In Kakaban's freshwater lake, reminiscent of the lake on Palau in

Opposite: *Sangalaki dive boats moored off the beach.*
Above: *Colourful Nudibranch or sea slug (Chromodoris bullocki) on a sea squirt (Polycarpa aurata).*

Micronesia, are four species of non-stinging jellyfish. What species these actually are is as yet unknown, although Dr Tomas Tomascik, a Canadian marine biologist working for the Indonesian Government, has done some work here. Borneo Divers has improved the track to the lake and supplies porters to carry your equipment, so you can dive as well as snorkel here.

Both islands are good for observing birds and butterflies, and at Sangalaki the circumstances are excellent for catching sight of turtles and turtle hatchlings. All the buildings are larger than those at Sipadan, but they are built well back from the beach and situated behind bushes so that their lights do not disturb turtles nesting at night. This, together with the fact that Borneo Divers has bought up the egg-collecting concession, means that on many nights 20–50 turtles come ashore to lay eggs, and turtle hatchlings are often seen. I soon learnt to carry a torch when I went to the restaurant at night in case I tripped over turtles on the way back to my chalet!

With a resort now set up at Pulau Derawan – a larger, inhabited island 50 minutes from Sangalaki – Pulau Derawan and Pulau Samama are also dived. Derawan is particularly good for night diving. Another good find is Maratua, with wild and testing conditions of strong currents but magnificent pelagic life and varied underwater topography. Maratua is an hour from Sangalaki by speedboat and must be dived at the right time of the tide to catch the current coming into the channel.

CURRENTS
The currents vary from medium to strong; their strength and direction depend on the tide at

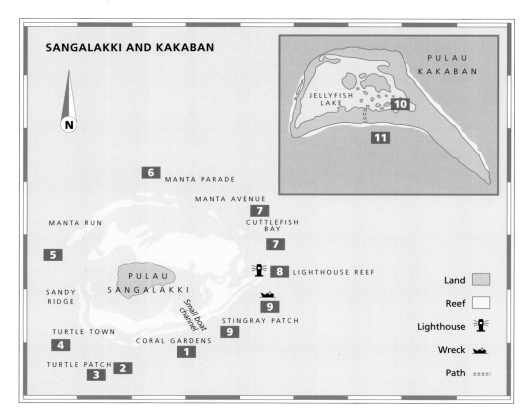

the time of your dive. Where they are strong, novices should stay beside the divemaster. Average visibility is almost everywhere about 30m (100ft).

A VARIETY OF MARINE LIFE

On almost every dive you can see Manta Rays, Eagle Rays, stingrays, cuttlefish, batfish, barracuda and Barramundi Cod, Coral Trout, groupers, many species of pufferfish, Spotted and Striped Sweetlips, hawkfish, Threadfin Bream, stonefish, damselfish, Anthias, Chromis and moray eels. Small sharks are around, usually Grey Reef, Whitetip Reef, Blacktip Reef and Leopard (Variegated). Also in evidence are shoals of fusiliers, snappers, catfish and jacks.

On the sand there are large barrel sponges covered with Alabaster Sea Cucumbers, as well as (truly giant) Giant Clams, some as much as 1m (40in) across, plus flat worms, fan worms, sea pens, sea stars, cushion stars, sea cucumbers, sea anemones (with and without clownfish), sponges and nudibranchs.

SANDY RIDGE

At Sandy Ridge there is a patch of Garden Eels. All around are isolated gorgonian sea fans, some very large and at remarkably shallow depths; these and many corals rising in the current are adorned with multicoloured feather stars. As well as large fields of stony corals, predominantly lettuce coral interspersed with boulder and brain coral, there are smaller fields of soft corals and many tube sponges.

The reef-fish fauna is as varied as at Sipadan but less concentrated; it includes Clown, Orangestriped and Titan Triggerfish, squirrelfish, surgeonfish and many species of angelfish and butterflyfish. There are remarkably few parrotfish, and those present are small.

The Yellow-saddle Goatfish (Parupeneus cyclostomus) uses the long whisker-like barbels on its chin to search for food in the sands. Goatfish usually forage in small groups.

1 CORAL GARDENS

★★★★★

Location: Just west outside the small boat channel.
Access: By boat, turning out of the small boat channel.
Conditions: Usually calm with a light current.
Average depth: 15m (50ft)
Maximum depth: 27m (90ft)
Mixed stony and soft corals shelve out gradually to 27m (90ft), after which there is flat sand. All the common Pacific reef fish, turtles, cuttlefish, nudibranchs, flat worms, sea stars, cushion stars, sea cucumbers, frogfish, lizardfish, goatfish and feather stars are in evidence.

2 DRIFTING FROM CORAL GARDENS TO TURTLE TOWN TO SANDY RIDGE

★★★★★

Location: The southwest area of the reef.
Access: By boat, turning west out of the small boat channel.
Conditions: Usually calm with a medium to strong current. Novices should stay with the divemaster.
Average depth: 24m (80ft)
Maximum depth: 28m (92ft)
The bottom here comprises an undulating expanse of stony corals, mostly vast fields of lettuce coral with some small soft corals, big whip corals and big gorgonian sea fans covered in feather stars. There are plenty of large shoals of fish, juvenile angelfish and butterflyfish, and all the expected Pacific reef fish, including Moorish Idols. Also in evidence are turtles, stingrays, groupers, small parrotfish, Barramundi Cod, sea stars, sea anemones, clownfish, cuttlefish and nudibranchs.

Outside this area is a field of large soft corals known as Sherwood Forest.

3 TURTLE PATCH

★★★★★

Location: At the southwest corner of the reef, between Turtle Town and Coral Gardens (see Site 2).
Access: By boat, west from the boat channel.
Conditions: Usually calm with a gentle current.
Average depth: 12m (40ft)
Maximum depth: 13m (43ft)
A level area of stony lettuce corals, with some large boulder corals forming overhangs that shelter many turtles. Some huge gorgonian sea fans are present at a depth of only 12m (40ft); you can see also lots of cuttlefish, Bandit and Porcupine Pufferfish and sea anemones with clown-

fish. In addition there are many leathery soft corals tinged with blue, all the expected reef fish, shoals of jacks and fusiliers, and, spread out on all the high points, feather stars.

4 TURTLE TOWN

★★★★★

Location: The southwest corner of the reef.
Access: By boat, west from the small boat channel.
Conditions: Usually calm with a light to medium current.
Average depth: 15m (50ft)
Maximum depth: 15m (50ft)
Here there are gullies and small ridges on stony coral in all directions. As the dive's name implies, there are lots of turtles. All the expected Pacific reef fish are here, too, along with sea stars and feather stars.

5 DRIFTING FROM MANTA RUN TO SANDY RIDGE

★★★★★

Location: The northwest to west area of the reef.
Access: By boat, either way around the island from the small boat channel.
Conditions: Generally calm but almost always some current, which can be strong. Novices should stay with the divemaster.
Average depth: 15m (50ft)
Maximum depth: 28m (92ft)
An undulating sandy bottom is dotted with coral heads, gorgonian sea fans and large barrel sponges. You can expect to see at least 20 Manta Rays in any one dive, and often these are curious enough to give you a close inspection. There are some patches of lettuce coral, individual *Dendronephthya* soft corals and sea anemones, sea cucumbers (many species) and sea stars, including cushion stars. There are also lots of small pufferfish, all the expected reef fish and many sea anemones (without attendant clownfish). There is a large patch of garden eels on Sandy Ridge by an old anchor.

6 MANTA PARADE

★★★★★

Location: The northernmost area of the reef.
Access: By boat from the small boat channel north around the east side of the reef.
Conditions: Generally calm but almost always some current, which can be strong. Novices should stay with the divemaster.

SINGAPORE

Many of the workaholics and expatriates who drive the dynamic economy of Singapore are also avid divers. These local enthusiasts are lucky enough to be at the hub of much of Southeast Asia's diving. Borneo, the southern islands of Peninsular Malaysia and the nearer dive sites of Indonesia can be easily reached for a weekend; and for longer breaks there is simple access to Indonesia's more distant dive sites as well as those in Thailand, the Philippines and Palau.

LIMITED VISIBILITY

However, the diving off Singapore itself is not good. The waters are shallow and there are heavy shipping movements and continuous construction projects which often involve land-fill reclamation of coastal waters. In short, the diving off the southern islands is best described (in the words of William Ong) as 'limited-visibility diving': a visibility of 1.5m (5ft) is considered a fine thing! The marine life is in fact pretty good – it is just difficult to see it. Surprises do occur; for example, a shoal of pink dolphins was observed between Pulau Tekong and Pulau Pengerang in April 1993, and dugongs sometimes show themselves in November by the fire jetty where the water fireboats are kept.

DANGEROUS CURRENTS

Many areas have strong and treacherous currents, and others are off-limits either for indus-trial reasons or because they are live-firing practice ranges. Nevertheless, a few areas are utilized for training novices or to allow more experienced divers to keep fit at weekends. Water temperatures average 27°C (81°F), and on a lucky day visibility can reach 5m (16ft), the best visibility occurring during the cooler months of October to April.

At weekends bumboats (converted lighters) depart from the Jardine Steps by the World Trade Centre around 08:00 taking picnickers, sunbathers, divers and snorkellers to Pulau Hantu, the Sisters Islands, St John's Island and Pulau Kusu.

Opposite: *The skyline of Singapore at night.*
Above: *Soft tree corals are a delightful sight in all Indo-Pacific waters.*

1 PULAU HANTU (GHOST ISLAND)

★★★★

Location: West–southwest of Pulau Bukom.

Access: By boat (about 45min) west–southwest from the Jardine Steps, around Sentosa Island and Pulau Bukom.

Conditions: Dive here only in calm conditions. Average visibility is about 1.2m (4ft).

Average depth: 12m (40ft)

Maximum depth: 15m (50ft)

This is Singapore's most popular location for diver training: a small island with patch reefs on the west side, which are sheltered from the main currents (though there are strong currents on the north side).

The fringing reef is made up of stony corals and rocks. A channel 12m (40ft) deep runs between the main island and the patch reefs, giving a choice of two slopes to a sandy bottom. There is some boulder coral, staghorn coral, lettuce coral, bubble coral, mushroom corals, encrusting corals and sponges, sea anemones (with clownfish), lionfish, scorpionfish, batfish, razorfish and feather stars. Down on the sand are sea stars, white and black sea urchins, sea cucumbers, nudibranchs, stingrays and gobies with alpheid shrimps. Turtles, sea snakes and sea horses are occasionally seen, and *Sargassum* may be found in the coldest season (October to February).

PULAU AUR

For better diving that is still relatively near home, Singapore Dive Operators now offer trips lasting 3—5 days to Pulau Aur (see page 84), off the east coast of Peninsular Malaysia, and to the Anambas archipelago, further east into Indonesian waters, where there are also convenient wrecks for wreck-diving courses.

Non-diving excursions go by fast ferry to the Indonesian island of Pulau Batam, which is about two-thirds the size of Singapore. With Singaporean help, Pulau Batam is fast becoming a 'second Singapore'.

---

2 PULAU SALU

★★★★

Location: West–southwest of the Jardine Steps, north of Pulau Sudong (Site 7).

Access: By boat (about 50min) west–southwest from the Jardine Steps.

Conditions: Dive here only in calm conditions. Novices should be wary: there can be strong currents. Average visibility is about 1.2m (4ft).

Average depth: 12m (40ft)

Maximum depth: 21m (70ft)

Pulau Salu is in a restricted area, but is dived for the

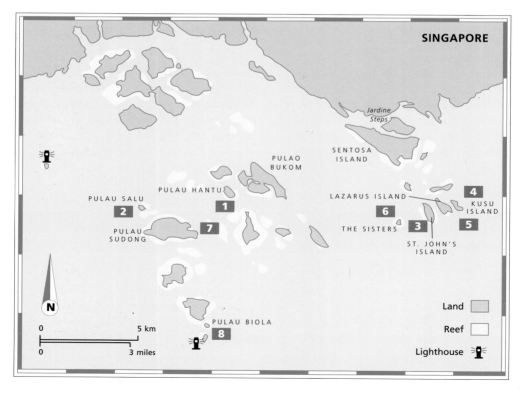

greater variety of marine life it offers than you can generally find elsewhere among Singapore's dive sites. There are good corals on the west side, and the western tip generally has the least current. Nurse Sharks have been seen on the reef.

3 ST JOHN'S ISLAND (PULAU SAKIJANG BENDERA; BARKING DEER ISLAND)
4 PULAU KUSU (TURTLE ISLAND)

★★★★

Location: Southeast of Sentosa Island.
Access: By boat (about 45min) from the Jardine Steps around and southeast of Sentosa Island.
Conditions: Dive at these sites only in calm conditions. There can be strong currents, so novices should not go out unescorted.
Average depth: 20m (65ft)
Maximum depth: 30m (100ft)
These are primarily tourist islands, and thus boast changing rooms and swimming lagoons. St John's is the larger of the two. Both islands have waters down to 30m (100ft), but the visibility is usually bad (1m; 40in). St John's has stony corals and the occasional pelagic fish or sea snake, while the reef on the northeast side of Pulau Kusu has some gorgonian sea fans, table corals and, occasionally, turtles.

5 PULAU LAZARUS

★★

Location: Between St John's Island and Pulau Kusu (Sites 3 and 4).
Access: By boat (about 45min) from the Jardine Steps around and southeast of Sentosa Island.
Conditions: Dive here only in calm conditions. The very strong currents that sometimes prevail make the site unsuitable for novices. Poor visibility: about 1m (40in).
Average depth: 15m (50ft)
Maximum depth: 18m (60ft)
This site, with its very strong currents, has little to recommend it except, on the southern tip, a wreck in 18m (60ft) of water.

6 SISTERS ISLANDS (PULAU SUBER LAUT)

★★★★

Location: South of Sentosa Island.
Access: By boat (about 45min) south from the Jardine Steps and around Sentosa Island.

Conditions: Dive here only in calm conditions. There can be some very strong currents, and only experienced divers should descend to the wreck. Average visibility is quite good for Singapore – at 1.5m (5ft)!
Average depth: 10m (33ft)
Maximum depth: 21m (70ft)
These two islands, west of St John's Island (Site 3), are close together and resemble each other in shape. There is a shallow reef at 6m (20ft) and the broken-up wreck of a steel barge in 21m (70ft) of water. Penetrating the wreck can be dangerous – divers have died in it. It is wise to inspect the wreck only from the outside.

7 PULAU SUDONG: EAST SIDE

★★

Location: West–southwest of the Jardine Steps, south of Pulau Hantu.
Access: By boat (about 45min) from the Jardine Steps and around Pulau Bukom.
Conditions: Dive here only in calm conditions. Novices should beware: there are very strong currents. Average visibility is poor: about 1m (40in).
Average depth: 9m (30ft)
Maximum depth: 20m (65ft)
The east side of Pulau Sudong is outside the restricted area but in the shipping lane. Currents are always strong. There is similar marine life to that at nearby Pulau Hantu (Site 1). About 150m (500ft) offshore to the north a beacon marks the wreck of a large steel barge on sand at 20m (65ft), with the deck at 9m (30ft). The wreck is mostly intact and has become a fine artificial reef, with excellent stony and soft corals. Fish fauna includes filefish – rare on the fringing reefs.

8 PULAU BIOLA (VIOLIN ISLAND) AND RAFFLES LIGHTHOUSE

★★

Location: Southwest of Sentosa Island.
Access: By boat (about 1hr) from the Jardine Steps and around Sentosa Island.
Conditions: Can be very rough, with big waves and heavy swells. Average visibility is poor: about 1m (40in).
Average depth: 34m (110ft)
Maximum depth: 34m (110ft)
The area between Pulau Pawai, Pulau Senang, Pulau Biola and Raffles Lighthouse is restricted for live-firing practice, and it has strong currents. Yet the area attracts experienced divers because it has better marine life than you can find elsewhere off Singapore. Local boatmen sink their old boats here, but these are mostly made of wood and so are unsafe to enter.

HOW TO GET THERE

Singapore is easily accessible by road or rail from Malaysia and Thailand, by ferry from Malaysia and Indonesia and by international flights from all over the world.

WHERE TO STAY

Upper Price Range
Raffles Hotel 1 Beach Road; tel 3371886/fax 3397650; e-mail raffles@raffles.com

Hilton International 581 Orchard Road; tel 7372233/fax 7322917

Shangri–La 22 Orange Grove Road; tel 7373644/fax 65-733-7220; e-mail sls@shangri-la.com

Medium Price Range
Hotel Bencoolen 47 Bencoolen Street; tel 3360822/fax 3364384

Hotel Peninsula 3 Coleman Street; tel 3372200

Metropolitan YMCA International Centre, 70 Palmer Road, Singapore 079427; tel 2224666/fax 2226467

Lower Price Range
South East Asia Hotel 190 Waterloo Street; tel 3382394/fax 3383480

WHERE TO EAT

There are restaurants of all standards and cuisines – too many to begin listing here.

DIVE FACILITIES

Singapore Underwater Federation Singapore Badminton Hall, 100 Guillemard Road Rm 5, Singapore 399718; tel 3444719/fax 3447803; e-mail sufnet@mbox3.singnet.com.sg. (Affiliated to the CMAS.)

Singapore Club Aquanaut (non-profit dive club), Block 512, #01-09, Chai Chee Lane, Bedok Industrial Estate, Singapore 469028; tel 4460155/fax 4495694; e-mail sca@bizlink.org.sg; www.sca.org.sg. PADI 5-star facility offering excursions to Malaysia and Indonesia.

Tech Diving Asia (TDI) tel 3398786/fax 3392276; e-mail info@tdiasia.com.sg; www.tdiasia.com.sg

Pro Diving Services (William & Ruby Ong) 32, Bali Lane (entrance via North Bridge Road, opposite the Landmark Hotel), Singapore 0718; tel 2912261/fax 2914136; e-mail prodiving@pacific.net.sg. PADI 5-star facility offering excursions to Malaysia and Indonesia.

Allround Sport Trading 105 Sims Avenue, #3-06 Chancerlodge Complex, Singapore 387429; tel 7492778/fax 7492977; e-mail allround@cyberway.co.sg; www.allround.com.sg. Retail outlet.

Asia Aquatic 55 Cuppage Road, #07-37 Cuppage Centre, Singapore 0922; tel 7388158/fax 7388153. Scuba travel.

Big Bubble Centre 68 Neil Road, Singapore 088836; tel 2226862/fax 2225751; e-mail bbcdiver@cyberway.com.sg; www.bigbubble.com. Scuba Travel and PADI sanctioned courses.

DiveMasters 315 Outram Road, #09-07 Tan Boon Liat Building, Singapore 169074; tel 2260991; e-mail divemstr@pacific.net.sg. Retail outlet.

Great Blue Dive Shop 211 Holland Avenue, #03-05 Holland Road, Shopping Centre, Singapore 1027; tel 4670767/fax 4696752

IANTD SE Asia (Koni Investment Pte. Ltd.), 196 Pandan Loop #06-17, Singapore 128384; tel 7767227/fax 7733239; e-mail khooss@singnet.com.sg; www.iantdsea.com. Technical diving training and equipment.

InnerSpace Dive Centre People's Park Centre, #05-49, 101 Upper Cross Street, Singapore 058357; tel 4382295/fax 4386955; e-mail innersdc@pacific.net.sg; www.innerspace.com.sg. PADI 5-star status.

IREI Singapore Pte Ltd 17 Rose Lane, Singapore 437377; tel 7482617/fax 7484972; e-mail admin@irei.com.sg; www.irei.com.sg. PADI 5-star IDC Centre.

Leeway Sub-Aquatic Paradise Block 115, #01-51, Aljunied Avenue 2, Singapore 1438; tel 7431208/fax 7453265. BS-AC School and retail outlet.

Mako Sub-Aquatics Block 71, Ayer Rajah Crescent #05-01, Ayer Rajah Industrial Park, Singapore 139951; tel 7741440/fax 7756935; e-mail mako@cyberway.com.sg; www.web.singnet.com.sg/~aloysius/makoonline/index.htm. NAUI courses to Divemaster.

Richmond Supplies & Services Pte. Ltd. 229 Beach Road B1-24, The Concourse Shopping Mall, Singapore 199554; tel 2950377; e-mail rmond@singnet.com.sg; www.web.singnet.com.sg. Retail outlet.

Scuba Corner 9 Raffles Boulevard, #02-47 Millenia Walk, Singapore 039596; tel 3386563/fax 3386931; e-mail scubacorner@scubacorner.com.sg; www.scubacorner.com.sg. PADI 5-star Dive Centre.

Scuba Diving Adventures (SDA) 61-B Pagoda Street, Singapore 059220; tel 2278317/fax 2265197; e-mail enquiry@scubada.com; www.scubada.com. Scuba travel and PADI courses.

Sentosa Water Sports Centre 1 Maritime Sq #01-06; tel 2745612/fax 2741087. Retail

outlet.

Sharkegg tel 95666591; e-mail sharkegg@mbox4.singnet.com.sg; www.web.singnet.com.sg/~sharkegg. PADI training to Advanced Open Water.

Vincent Dive Centre Block 212 #04-265 Bishan Street 23, Singapore 570212, tel 5523544/fax 5523550; e-mail vincediv@pacific.net.sg; www.vincentdive.com. PADI training plus MV *Vincent* live-aboard trips to Malaysia and Indonesia.

Sentosa Water Sports World Trade Centre #1–6, 1 Maritime Square; tel 2745612/fax 2741087

Mako Sub-Aquatics #05–01/03, 71 Ayer Rajah Crescent; tel 7741440

Great Blue Dive Shop Holland Road Shopping Centre, 211 Holland Avenue #03–05, Singapore 1027; tel 4670767/fax 4696752. NAUI courses and excursions.

Underwater Photographic Equipment
Andrew Yeo #02–15 The Adelphi, 1 Coleman Street, Singapore 0617; tel 3376334/fax 3391869; e-mail seansea@pacific.net.sg. Aquaflash, Sea & Sea, Anthis Nexus and Subal.

DiveMasters Pratama Pte. Ltd. 315 Outram Road, #09-07 Tan Boon Liat Building, Singapore 69074; tel 2260994/fax 2273983. Underwater photography & scuba equipment.

Singapore Scuba Photo & Equipment Centre 1 Scotts Road #03-48, Shaw Centre, Singapore 228208; tel 7325582/fax 7320817; e-mail chrissc@pacific.net.sg. Underwater photography & scuba equipment.

LIVE-ABOARD BOATS

Although not well advertised, some live-aboard have departures from Singapore. The MV *Empress* covers Indonesia, is a BSAC School and is often chartered for scientific expeditions or surveys, while the MV *Mata Ikan* covers technical diving, including deep wrecks such as the HMS *Prince of Wales* and HMS *Repulse* and is a TDI training facility.

MV *Empress* 14 Hyde Park Gate, Selatar Air Base, Singapore 799543; tel 4825354/fax 4844143; e-mail vidar@swiftech.com.sg; www.tdiasia.com.sg; http://blackbox.swiftech.net.sg/~vidar

MV _Mata Ikan_ Tech Diving Asia; fax 3392276; e-mail info@tdiasia.com.sg

MV _Vincent_ Vincent Dive Centre, Block 212 #04-265 Bishan Street 23, Singapore 570212; tel 5523544/fax 5523550; e-mail vincediv@ pacific.net.sg; www.vincentdive.com

FILM PROCESSING

E6 transparency processing is handled by the following laboratories:

RGB
01-01 Premier Centre, 103 Beach Road, Singapore 189704; tel 3346146
and
01-01 Wellington Building, 20 Bideford Road, Singapore 229921; tel 7383168
and
Kallang Avenue Premier Centre, Beach Rd
and
Winsland House II, Penang Rd. A Kodak Q-lab well known for its E6 processing, RGB can turn around films in around 3 hours.

KJ Colourlab & Studio 302 Tiong Bahru Road, #02-22 Tiong Bahru Plaza, Singapore 168732; tel 2727706/fax 2727071

HOSPITALS AND RECOMPRESSION CHAMBER

Singapore General Hospital Outram Road; tel 2223322

Glen Eagles Hospital tel 4737222

Mount Elizabeth Hospital tel 7372666

Recompression (Hyperbaric) Chamber
Office of Chief Navy Medical Officer, Republic of Singapore Navy, AFPN 6060 Sembawang Camp, Admiralty Road West, Singapore 759960; tel (65) 7505544/fax (65) 7505610. Three multiple occupancy hyperbaric chambers and two single-occupancy chambers.

LOCAL HIGHLIGHTS

Singapore is a cosmopolitan city, with Chinese, Arab and Indian areas.

A wide range of **cruises** operate on the Singapore River, around the harbour and to nearby islands.

The main shopping district is in the vicinity of **Orchard Road**; while here you can visit the famous **Raffles Hotel**. Other places to visit include **Chinatown, Little India** and **Arab Street, St Andrew's Cathedral,** the **Thian Hock Keng Temple,** the **Kong Meng San Phor Kark See Temple,** the **Sri Mariamman Temple,** the **Temple of 1000 Lights,** the **Siong Lim Temple,** the **Sultan Mosque,** the **Al-Abrar Mosque** and the **Hajjah Fatimah Mosque**. Then, as if that were not enough, there are the **National Museum and Art Gallery**, the many gardens, the **Jurong Bird Park and Crocodile Park,** the zoo and the mythologically based _**Merlion Statue**_. **Sentosa Island,** a UK military base until 1970, is now one large theme park. You can cross to Sentosa by one of the regular ferries, but a better deal is to buy an all-in ticket

at the cable-car station by the World Trade Centre: this gives you not only the cable-car ride to the summit of **Faber Mountain**, Singapore's highest point, but also buses and the monorail on Sentosa Island and entrance to several of the attractions there.

Bantayan (Eye-patch) Butterflyfish (Chaetodon adiergastos) tend to stay with the same partner until one dies.

CONSERVATION IN MALAYSIA

The main causes of reef destruction in Malaysia are removal of coral for building, damage caused by blast fishing or trawlers getting too close to reefs, river run-off, and effluent and sewage discharge into the sea.

Blast fishing, illegal since 1985, has been curbed to some extent, but still continues in a few areas. How much damage has been caused by sedimentation is not really known, but in Peninsular Malaysia it has been noticeable around Pangkor and the Sembilan Islands and in the Pulau Perhentian and Pulau Redang groups. In Sabah, sedimentation damage has occurred in the Tunku Abdul Rahman Marine Park and around Kota Kinabalu.

Malaysian reefs and adjacent waters are important for both subsistence and commercial fishing, and in some areas reef fish comprise as much as 30% of the total fish catch. As with other countries, there has been a marked decline in fisheries in certain areas (e.g., the Strait of Malacca), and populations of marine turtles have declined throughout.

Providing long-term protection for coral reefs is a complex task, since it is not only a question of protecting the reef itself but also of ensuring that nearby land-based activities do not adversely affect the corals and marine life. Marine parks are often only really effective if part of a coastal-management programme that also encompasses terrestrial habitats. Thus the integration of protected areas requires considerable resources as well as commitment on the part of national governments.

Another important component of coral-reef conservation is the use of Environmental Impact Assessment (EIA) studies, which help pinpoint potential problem areas in the development of coastal regions. Finally, community involvement and public education are vital if the need for sustainable management is to be understood and carried through at local level.

The Malaysian government has recognized the need for integrated planning and management of both land and sea to control and minimize adverse effects on the marine environment. About 25 Marine Protected Areas (MPAs) are either planned or already in existence. In terms of public education and, just as important, the provision of improved economic opportunities (so that no one need damage reefs to sustain their livelihood), several government agencies and NGOs are active in the community. Despite the government's commitment to marine conservation, there are major challenges to be faced. EIAs are mandatory in Malaysian law for only some development projects, and there are many shortcomings in the procedures which will need rectification if they are to become truly effective. Planning at the regional level often fails to incorporate environmental criteria, and it can take up to four years to implement management plans even when agreed upon. Securing consensus between the different levels of government is another problem, since political approval for conservation measures also has to be gained at local and state level. Finally, trained marine personnel are in short supply.

The growth of sport diving in Malaysia provides a powerful economic incentive to improve the effectiveness of marine-conservation measures and, ultimately, a sustainable future for the country's marine heritage.

CONSERVATION IN SINGAPORE

The recent history of Singapore is one of continuous construction, particularly on the southern coast and the southern islands. Inland construction projects deposit silt into the rivers and hence the sea, while coastal construction projects are mostly on land reclaimed using landfill. Many thousands of tonnes of sand have been used to make the artificial beaches of Sentosa Island. The level of siltation is exacerbated by regular construction on the nearby Indonesian islands, busy shipping movements and industrial pollution.

Fortunately Singapore has some very vociferous and active conservation societies, both marine and terrestrial. The Republic of Singapore Yacht Club, the Singapore Underwater Federation and the Singapore Institute of Biology, supported by the Singapore Sea Sports Liaison Committee, spent four years making extensive surveys of Singapore's coral reefs, using hundreds of volunteer divers. They presented a comprehensive report to the government in 1991. The Marine Conservation Group of the Malayan Nature Society (Singapore Branch) recently organized the transplantation of corals from threatened reefs to an area of Sentosa Island where no reef existed. This 'coral-reef rescue project' was sponsored by the Care-for-Nature Trust Fund and the Hong Kong Bank. The key organizer was marine biologist Helen Newman, with the help of volunteer divers from local dive clubs, dive shops and universities.

Opinions vary about this type of project. Some say that often the wrong types of corals for the site might be transplanted and would soon die, so it would have been better to install an artificial reef. However, the transplanted corals have been constantly monitored and scientific knowledge gained. The ensuing publicity has done much to develop public awareness, and another similar project is now under way – to transplant to Sentosa Island the corals of Pulau Air Chawan, off Jurong.

COMMON FISH

Angelfish (family Pomacanthidae)
These beautiful fish, with their minute, brushlike teeth, browse on sponges, algae and corals. Their vibrant colouring varies according to the species, like those of the butterflyfish and were once thought part of the same family. However, they are distinguishable by a short spike extending from the gill cover. Angelfish are territorial in habit and tend to occupy the same caves or ledges for a period of time.

Emperor Angelfish, 30cm (12in)
Pomancanthus Imperator

Barracuda (family Sphyraenidae)
With their elongated, streamlined, silvery body and sinister-looking jaws, barracudas tend to appear rather fearsome. However, even though they rarely threaten divers, caution on approach is advisable. Barracudas are effective reef predators. They tend to school in large numbers when young but by the time they mature to a length of two metres or longer, they prefer to hunt singly or in pairs.

Pickhandle Barracuda, 2m (6½ft)
Sphyraena Jello (& Remora)

Bigeyes (family Priacanthidae)
As their name suggests, these small, nocturnal fish have extremely large eyes. Bigeyes are effective predators which hide in protective holes in the coral by day and venture out at night to feed on other small fish, crabs, larvae and the larger planktonic animals (the organic life which is found floating at various depths.

Big Eye, 30cm (12in)
Priacanthus Hamrur

Blenny (family Blenniidae)
Blennies are often incredibly hard to spot, since they are usually well camouflaged and blend into the rubble- or algae-covered reef bottom where they live. The carnivorous blennies are ferocious hunters; whipping out so quickly from their hiding places to snatch small prey that the entire split-second action can go completely unnoticed unless you know exactly what you're looking for and where to look.

Blenny, 15cm (6in)
Blennidae

Butterflyfish (family Chaetodontidae)
Among the most colourful of reef inhabitants, butterflyfish have flat, thin bodies, usually with a stripe through the eye and sometimes with a dark blotch near the tail: this serves as camouflage and confuses predators, who lunge for the wrong end of the fish. Butterflyfish can also, unusually, swim backwards to escape danger. Many species live as mated pairs and have territories while others school in large numbers.

Racoon Butterflyfish, 21cm (8in)
Chaetodon Lunula

Damselfish and Clownfish (family Pomacentridae)
These pugnacious little fish often farm their own patch of algae. Found almost everywhere on the reef, they also sometimes form large aggregations to feed on plankton. Clownfishes (*Amphiprion spp*) and *Premnas Biaculeatus*, which live among the stinging tentacles of the sea anemone, are also members of this family. Of the 27 clownfish species known from the Indo-Pacific, 15 are found on the reefs of Southeast Asia.

Clownfish, 5cm (2in)
Amphiprion Rubrocinctus

Cardinalfish (family Apogonidae)
These tiny fish live in a wide range of depths down the reef. Their colours vary widely, but most have large eyes which help their night vision as they come out of hiding to feed on the plankton that rises up through the water as night falls. Cardinalfish also have large mouths and, in some species,

Largetooth Cardinal Fish, 12cm (5in)
Cheilodipterus Macrodon

the male incubates the eggs inside its mouth. During this period, the male juggles the egg mass from time to time and refrains from feeding. This process is known as mouth brooding and is a reproductive strategy that is used by certain species of marine fish.

Goatfish (family Mullidae)
Easily recognized by their chin whiskers, a pair of long barbels which they use to hunt for food, goatfish are often seen moving along sandflats, stirring up small clouds of sand as they feel beneath the surface for prey. They sometimes forage in small groups or large schools. Goatfish are benthic, or 'bottom dwellers', which is the name for fish that either feed or lie camouflaged on the ocean floor.

Yellowsaddle Goatfish, 25-30cm (10-12in)
Parupeneus Cyclostomus

Goby (family Gobiidae)
The Goby is another 'bottom dweller' which can remain undetected on the sea bed for long periods of time. They have large, protruding eyes which are raised above the level of the head and powerful jaws which enable them to snatch prey and dart back to safety. Gobies are among the most successful reef families, with literally hundreds of species. Their colouring varies from brightly coloured to quite drab.

Hector's Goby, 15cm (6in)
Amblygobius Hectori

Grouper (family Serranidae)
Groupers range from just a few centimetres long to the massive Giant Grouper, 3.5m (12ft) long. They vary enormously in colour; grey with darker spots is the most common. Movement is slow except when attacking prey with remarkable speed. All groupers are carnivorous, feeding on invertebrates and other fish. Like wrasse and parrotfish, some start out as females and become males later while others are hermaphroditic.

Lunartail Grouper, 35cm (14in)
Variola Louti

Jack and Trevally (family Carangidae)
Jacks and trevallies are fast predators which range in size from small to very large. they can be silver, black, green or yellow. They are usually found in the open water but are occasional visitors to the reef since they follow the current as they feed. Cruising the outer slopes, they dash in with lightning speed to snatch unwary reef fish. They can be seen singly, schooling or in small groups.

Yellowspotted Jack Fish, 30cm (12in)
Carangoides Fulvoguttatus

Moray Eel (family Muraenidae)
This ancient species of fish have gained their undeserved reputation for ferocity largely because, as they breathe, they open and close the mouth to reveal their numerous sharp teeth. They do not have fins or scales. Moray Eels anchor the rear portion of their bodies in a selected coral crevice and stay hidden during the day. They emerge at night to feed on shrimp, octopuses and mussels and are immediately attracted by the smell of dead or injured fish.

Giant Moray Eel, 2m (6½ft)
Gymnothorax Javanicus

Moorish Idol (family Zanclidae)
This graceful and flamboyant fish reaches a maximum size of 20cm. It is easily distinguished by its long dorsal fin, thick protuding lips and pointed snout. It probes for food (mostly algae and invertebrates) in nooks and crannies. Moorish Idols are usually seen individually, but may sometimes form large aggregations prior to spawning. Moorish Idols are related to surgeonfish even though their body shape is quite different.

Moorish Idol, 18cm (7in)
Zanclus Cornutus

Parrotfish (family Scaridae)
So-called because of their sharp, parrot-like beaks and bright colours, the parrotfishes are among the most important herbivores on the reef. Many change colour and sex as they grow, the terminal-phase males developing striking coloration by comparison with the drabness of the initial-phase males and females. Many build trans-

parent cocoons of mucus to sleep in at night, the mucus acting as a scent barrier against predators. The beak of the Parrotfish enable them to crunch the surface of coral rock to feed on algal stubble and boring algae within.

Swarthy Parrotfish, 40cm (16cm)
Scarus Niger

Pipefish and Seahorse (family Syngathidae)
Pipefish and seahorses, are poor swimmers. They tend to lurk in seagrass beds or amongst coral away from currents. Seahorses use their tails to wrap themselves around corals and seagrasses to stop themselves being swept away. Their vulnerability has forced them to become masters of disguise, some-times mimicking a blade of grass or a gorgonian coral.

Pipefish, 14cm (5½in)
Corythoichthys

Pufferfish (family Tetraodontidae)
These small to medium-size, highly poisonous, omnivores feed on algae, worms, molluscs and crustaceans. Pufferfish are found all the way down the reef to depths of around 30m (100ft). They are slow moving but when threatened, they inflate themselves into big, round balls by sucking water into the abdomen, so that it becomes almost an impossible task for predators to try and swallow them.

Map Pufferfish, 50cm (20in)
Arothron Mappa

Snapper (family Lutjanidae)
Snappers are important carnivores on the reef, feeding mostly at night. Many are inshore-dwellers, although the Yellowtail Snapper is a midwater fish and the commer-cially exploited Red Snapper dwells most at depths. Snappers are becoming much rarer on the reefs because they are

Checkered Snapper, 22cm (9in)
Lutjanus Decussatus

long-lived and slow-growing which means that once the populations are drastically reduced they unfortunately take a long time to replenish.

Soldierfish and Squirrelfish (family Holocentridae)
Both species are nocturnal fish and are often confused with each other. Soldierfish have a rounder, bulkier body and are more evenly coloured than squirrelfish. The red or reddish-orange coloration and large eyes are also com-mon among other nocturnal fishes like bigeyes. Dozing under rocks or corals by day, they emerge by night to feed. They have serrated, spiny scales and sharp defensive fins. They lack the preopercu-lar spine.

Blotch Eye Soldierfish, 12cm (5in)
Myripristis Murdjan

Triggerfish (family Balistidae)
Triggerfish are medium to large fish with flattened bodies and often striking markings (e.g., the Picasso Triggerfish [*Rhinecanthus aculeatus*]), these have powerful teeth and feed on crustaceans and echinoderms on the mid-reef. Large species cruise coral looking for food. When a trig-gerfish is threat-ened it squeezes itself into a crevice and erects its first dorsal spine, lock-ing it into place with a second, smaller spine: this stays wedged until the 'trigger' is released.

Orangestriped Triggerfish, 18cm (7in)
Balistapus Undulatus

Wrasse and Hogfish (family Labridae)
Wrasse vary enormously in size, from the tiny Cleaner Wrasse (*Labroides spp*) to the giant Napoleon Wrasse (*Cheilinus undulatus*), which can reach nearly 2m (6½ft) in length. Wrasse are usually brightly coloured and go through various colour and sex changes as they mature. Their distinctive buck teeth are well adapted to pulling molluscs from rocks or picking off crus-taceans. Most live in shallow reef areas, although some will frequent greater depths.

Giant Humphead Wrasse, 1m (40in)
Cheilinus Undulatus

UNDERWATER PHOTOGRAPHY

Underwater photography requires a good deal of preparation before entering the water. You cannot change prime lenses underwater, so it's important to establish what you wish to photograph before you take the plunge, in order to get the best results. There is the possibility of using a zoom lens on a housed camera or a Nikonos RS-AF, which gives a degree of extra flexibility, but zoom lenses can lack sharpness. If the water is calm you can carry two camera outfits, one for wide-angle and another for close-up or macro.

DEDICATED UNDERWATER CAMERAS

The Nikonos V and the Sea & Sea Motor Marine II are both non-reflex waterproof cameras with Through-The-Lens (TTL) automatic exposure systems with dedicated flash guns. In stronger currents the Nikonos V is easier to handle. Nikonos lenses range from 15mm to 80mm in focal length: the 35mm and 80mm lenses can be used in air, and are really only useful underwater when fitted to extension tubes or close-up outfits; the 28mm lens should be considered as the standard lens.

Independent companies supply lenses, lens converters, extension tubes and a housing for fish-eye and superwide land camera lenses to fit the Nikonos. Lens converters are particularly convenient as they can be changed underwater. The Motor Marine II, for example, makes good use of these, with converters for wide-angle and macro. The Nikonos close-up kit can also be changed underwater. The specially designed Nikonos lenses give sharper results underwater than any housed camera, though the lack of reflex focusing makes it difficult to compose pictures and it is easy to cut off part of a subject. Remember that the focusing scale on the 35mm and 80mm is inscribed in 'in-air' distances, while that on the 15mm, 20mm and 28mm underwater lenses is inscribed in underwater distances.

The now-discontinued Nikonos RS-AF is a fully waterproof reflex camera with autofocus, dedicated lenses and a dedicated flash gun. It is very heavy. Its high price makes it a poor buy in comparison with housed high-specification land cameras, which are more versatile, weigh less, are cheaper to replace when flooded and can be used on land.

HOUSED CAMERAS

Land cameras can be used underwater in specialist metal or Plexiglas housings. These are available for top-grade reflex cameras. There are advantages and disadvantages to each system. Metal housings are strong, reliable, work well at depth and will last a long time if properly maintained. However, they can be heavy to carry – though they do have buoyancy in water. Their higher cost is justified if one is using an expensive camera that deserves the extra protection.

Plexiglas housings are cheaper but more fragile and require careful handling, both above and below the water. Some models compress at depth, making the control rods miss the camera controls. These control rods can be adjusted to work at depths, but then do not function properly near to the surface. Most underwater photographs are taken near to the surface, so this drawback is not serious. These housings are lightweight to carry on land, but often too buoyant in the water where you have to attach extra weights to them.

'O' Rings and Other Equipment

Underwater cameras, housings, flash guns and cables have 'O' ring seals. These and their mating surfaces or grooves must be kept scrupulously clean. 'O' rings should be lightly greased with silicone grease to prevent flooding (the Nikonos RS-AF uses a different grease). Too much grease will attract grit and hairs. Silicone spray should not be used, as its cooling effect causes 'O' rings to crack. When not in use, it is best to store any user-removable 'O' rings off the unit to avoid them becoming flattened. The unit itself should then be sealed in a plastic bag to keep out moisture. User-removable 'O' rings on Nikonos cameras and flash synchronization cables are best replaced every 12 months. Non-user-removable 'O' rings should be serviced every 12–18 months. As a general rule, those on housings usually last the life of the housing.

Note that housings without controls, which are designed for fully auto cameras, require fast films to obtain reasonable shutter speeds and lens apertures in the low ambient light underwater. Autofocus systems that work on contrast (not infrared) work underwater but only on high contrast subjects – not on those that have large areas of one colour.

PHOTOGRAPHIC TIPS

Point-and-shoot does not work – get closer than arm's length and make sure the subject fills more than half of the frame. Wide-angle close-up shots have impact.

Limit people shots to head and shoulders, unless you have very wide-angle lenses. For smaller creatures use macro lenses, close-up kits or extension tubes with framers.

Wherever possible do not aim the camera down, but aim it horizontally or better still upwards, otherwise the background in the picture will be dark.

Keep film in its individual sealed containers until you use it.

If you must buy film locally, buy it in a respected photography outlet or major hotel, where it will have spent most of its storage life in cool conditions.

If you keep film refrigerated, give it at least two hours to defrost before loading it in a camera.

Do not assemble underwater cameras or housings in cool air-conditioned rooms or cabins; you are likely to get condensation inside them when you then take them into the water.

Normal cameras that have been in air-conditioned rooms, cabins or vehicles will mist up when taken out into a warm atmosphere. You will have to wait at least ten minutes for the condensation to evaporate before you can take any clear photographs.

When balancing flash with daylight, cameras with faster flash synchronization speeds, 1/125 or 1/250 second, give sharper results by avoiding the double images associated with fast moving fish.

Masks hold your eyes away from the viewfinder, so buy the smallest volume mask you can wear. Cameras fitted with optical action finders or eyepiece magnifiers are useful in housings but this is not so important with autofocus systems.

Light refraction through your mask and through the camera lens causes objects to appear one-third closer and larger than in air. Reflex focusing or visually estimated distances remain correct, but if you measure distances by a ruler, these must be reduced by one-third when setting the lens focus if it is inscribed in 'in-air' distances.

With a flat port (window), in front of the lens, refraction increases the focal length of the lens and decreases its sharpness, due to the individual colours of light being refracted at different angles and speeds (chromatic aberration). This is most pronounced with wide-angle lenses, which should be corrected by using a convex dome port. Dome ports require lenses to be able to focus on a virtual image at around 30cm (1ft), so you may have to fit supplementary positive dioptre lenses to some camera lenses.

FLASH

Water acts as a cyan (blue/green) filter, cutting back red, so colour film will have a blue/green cast. For available light photography, different filters are sold to correct this in either cold or tropical waters, but they reduce the already limited amount of light available. Flash will put back the colour and increase apparent sharpness.

Modern flash guns have TTL automatic exposure systems. Underwater, large flash guns have good wide-angle performance usable up to 1.5m (5ft). Smaller flash guns have a narrow angle and only work up to 1m (40 inches) – diffusers widen the angle covered, but you lose at least one F-stop in output. Some land flash guns are more advanced than most underwater flash guns, and can be housed for underwater use.

Flash guns used on or near to the camera will light up suspended matter in the water like white stars in a black sky (back scatter). The closer these particles are to the camera, the larger they will appear. The solution is to keep the flash as far as possible above and to one side of the camera. Two narrow-angle flash guns, one on each side of the camera, often produce a better result than a single wide-angle flash gun.

When photographing divers, remember the golden rule that the eyes within the mask must be lit and in focus. Flash guns with a colour temperature of 4500° Kelvin will give more accurate skin tones and colour.

In a multiple flash set-up the prime flash gun will meter by TTL if this is available and (unless it has TTL-Slave) any other flash gun connected will give its pre-programmed output, so this should be set low to achieve modelling light. TTL-Slaves should have a lower output than the main flash for the same reason.

Multiple segment matrix flash exists with some housed cameras connected to housed matrix flash guns. With

---

THE ADVANCED PHOTO SYSTEM

Some SLRs and compact cameras are available in the Advanced Photo System (APS). Film cassettes have symbols indicating whether the film is unexposed, partially exposed, or fully exposed or whether they have been processed. Fully exposed or processed films are automatically rejected and the camera cannot be opened unless the film is rewound. With higher specification cameras, the film can be rewound and changed mid-film in air.

Three image formats are possible in-camera on the same film: 'C', Classic has the standard 2:3 aspect ratio; 'H', HDTV for group and wide shots has a 9:16 aspect ratio; and 'P', Panoramic has a 1:3 aspect ratio. A magnetic strip on the film records the selected picture size, and APS processing equipment uses this data to make frame-by-frame adjustments to optimize each photograph.

---

other TTL systems, although the ambient light metering may be multiple segment matrix, the flash metering is by a single segment in the centre of the frame. This means that flash on smaller off-centre foreground subjects may not be correctly metered with these systems.

Although objects appear closer to both your eye and the camera lens under water, the flash must strike the subject directly to illuminate it. Narrow-angle flash guns must therefore be aimed behind the apparent subject, to hit the real subject. Built-in aiming/focusing lights, or a torch strapped to the flash, aid both this problem and focusing during night photography. Built-in aiming/focusing lights are best powered by a separate battery, or the system will not last for a complete dive.

Fish scales reflect light in different ways that vary with the angle of the fish to the camera. Silver fish reflect more light than coloured fish and black fish almost none at all – therefore you should bracket exposures. With automatic flash guns you do this by altering the film speed setting.

The easiest way to balance flash with available light is to use TTL flash with a camera on aperture priority metering. Take a meter reading of the mid-water background that agrees with your chosen flash synchronization speed, set your flash to TTL and it will correctly light your subject. If you do not have multi-segment matrix flash then your subject should be in the central part of the frame. If you use manual exposure, using an aperture half a stop higher than the meter recommends will give a darker background and make the subject stand out more.

If possible bracket your exposures by altering the film speed. At distances of less than 1m (40 inches) most automatic flash guns tend to overexpose, so allow for this.

FILM

For black and white photography, fast 400 ISO film is the first choice. For a beginner wishing to use colour, negative print film is best, offering plenty of exposure latitude. Reversal film is preferred for reproduction, but requires very accurate exposure.

Kodachrome films are ideal for close work but with mid-water shots they produce a blue/green water background – although this is accurate, people are conditioned to a 'blue' sea. Ektachrome and Fujichrome produce blue water backgrounds; 50–100 ISO films are the best compromise between exposures and grain. Pale yellow filters will cut down the blue.

Kodak's Underwater Ektachrome would be very useful for coral and large subjects such as shipwrecks, whale sharks and manta rays if only it had a film speed of 200 ISO or greater. As it is, with a film speed of 50 ISO, its uses are limited in the low light levels prevalent underwater.

Push/Pull Processing

Colour negative films have an exposure latitude of up to four stops and black-and-white films have even more, but colour transparency films should be exposed to within a quarter of a stop of the correct value.

If you have been on holiday or on a longer trip there is always the possibility that cameras, flash guns and meters have not behaved correctly. Processors anywhere can suffer problems from power cuts or machinery failure, so professional photographers never have all their exposed film processed at the same time; instead they process it in small batches. This has the advantage that you can review the results of the films processed. If all is not right, E6 process films can have their processing adjusted by professional processing laboratories, who can 'push' them by up to two stops faster or 'pull' them back by one stop slower. There will be some change in colour and contrast but not a lot.

Kodachrome film can be adjusted to a lesser extent by laboratories in the USA or Kodak's Professional Laboratory at Wimbledon in the UK.

If you have any doubts about a particular film you can have a 'clip test' done; the first few frames are cut off and processed separately first, then the rest of the film is processed according to the results of the clip test.

PHOTOGRAPHIC SUBJECTS

What you photograph depends on your personal interests. Macro photography with extension tubes and fixed framers is easiest to get right: the lens-to-subject distance and flash-to-subject distance are fixed, and the water sediment is minimized. Expose a test film at a variety of exposures with a fixed set-up and the best result will be the exposure to use for all future pictures for this setting and film.

Some fish are strongly territorial. Surgeonfish, triggerfish and sharks will make mock attacks on a perceived invader and these situations can make strong pictures if you are brave enough to hold your ground. Manta rays are curious and will keep coming back if you react quietly and do not chase after them. Angelfish and butterflyfish will swim off when you first enter their territory, but if you remain quietly in the same place they will usually return and allow you to photograph them. Remember that if an eye is in the picture it must be lit and sharp, it is acceptable for the rest of the animal to be slightly blurred.

Diver and wreck photography are the most difficult. Even with apparently clear water and wide-angle lenses there will be back scatter, and flash is essential to light a diver's mask. Note that when the sun is at a low angle, or in choppy seas, much of the light fails to enter the water. To take advantage of the maximum light available it is best to photograph two hours either side of the sun's highest point. Sunlight can give spectacular effects underwater, especially in silhouette shots, though generally you should keep the sun behind you and on your subject.

Night photography underwater is another world. Focusing quickly in dim light is difficult and many subjects will disappear when lit up, so pre-set the controls. Many creatures only appear at night and some fish are half asleep, making them more approachable.

For all kinds of photography, good buoyancy control is essential. Remember not to touch coral and do not wear fins over sandy bottoms, as they will stir sand up.

Batteries

A major problem for travelling photographers is keeping up with battery charging. If your equipment can use AA or D cell batteries, these will be available at most mainland towns, though they may be old or stored in bad conditions. If you can carry the weight it is best to take a fresh supply with you.

Health and Safety for Divers

The information in this section is intended as a guide only, it is no substitute for thorough training or professional medical advice. The information is based on currently accepted health and safety information but it is certainly not meant to be a substitute for a comprehensive manual on the subject. We strongly advise that the reader obtains a recognised manual on diving safety and medicine before embarking on a trip.

- Divers who have suffered any injury or symptom of an injury, no matter how minor, related to diving, should consult a doctor, preferably a specialist in diving medicine, as soon as possible after the symptom or injury occurs.

- No matter how confident you are in formulating your own diagnosis remember that you remain an amateur diver and an amateur doctor.
- If you yourself are the victim of a diving injury do not be shy to reveal your symptoms at the expense of ridicule. Mild symptoms can later develop into a major illness with life threatening consequences. It is better to be honest with yourself and live to dive another day.
- Always err on the conservative side when considering your ailment, if you discover you only have a minor illness both you and the doctor will be relieved.

GENERAL PRINCIPLES OF FIRST AID

The basic principles of first aid are:
• doing no harm
• sustaining life
• preventing deterioration
• promoting recovery

In the event of any illness or injury a simple sequence of patient assessment and management can be followed. The sequence first involves assessment and definition of any life threatening conditions followed by management of the problems found.

The first thing to do is to ensure both the patient's and your own safety by removing yourselves from the threatening environment. Make sure that whatever your actions, they in no way further endanger the patient or yourself.

Then the first things to check are:
• A : for AIRWAY (with care of the neck)
• B : for BREATHING
• C : for CIRCULATION
• D : for DECREASED level of consciousness
• E : for EXPOSURE (the patient must be adequately exposed in order to examine them properly)

• **Airway (with attention to the neck):** - is there a neck injury? Is the mouth and nose free of obstruction? Noisy breathing is a sign of airway obstruction.
• **Breathing:** Look at the chest to see if it is rising and falling. Listen for air movement at the nose and mouth. Feel for the movement of air against your cheek.
• **Circulation:** Feel for a pulse next to the wind pipe (carotid artery)
• **Decreased level of consciousness:** Does the patient respond in any of the following ways:
    A - Awake, Aware, Spontaneous speech
    V - Verbal Stimuli, does he answer to 'Wake up!'
    P - Painful Stimuli, does he respond to a pinch
    U - Unresponsive
• **Exposure:** Preserve the dignity of the patient as far as possible but remove clothes as necessary to adequately effect your treatment.

Now, send for help
If you think the condition of the patient is serious following your assessment, you need to send or call for help from the emergency services (ambulance, paramedics). Whoever you send for help must come back and tell you that help is on its way.

Recovery Position
If the patient is unconscious but breathing normally there is a risk of vomiting and subsequent choking on their own vomit. It is therefore critical that the patient be turned onto his/her side in the recovery position. If you suspect a spinal or neck injury, be sure to immobilize the patient in a straight line before you turn him/her on his/her side.

Cardiopulmonary Resuscitation (CPR)
Cardiopulmonary Resuscitation is required when the patient is found to have no pulse. It consists of techniques to:
• ventilate the patient's lungs - expired air resuscitation
• pump the patient's heart - external cardiac compression

Once you have checked the ABC's you need to do the following:

Airway
Open the airway by gently extending the head (head tilt) and lifting the chin with two fingers (chin lift). This will lift the tongue away from the back of the throat and open the airway. If you suspect a foreign body in the airway sweep your finger across the back of the tongue from one side to the other. If one is found, remove it. Do not attempt this is in a conscious or semi-conscious patient as they will either bite your finger off or vomit.

Breathing
• If the patient is not breathing you need to give expired air resuscitation, in other words you need to breath air into their lungs.
• Pinch the patient's nose closed.
• Place your mouth, open, fully over the patient's mouth, making as good a seal as possible.
• Exhale into the patient's mouth hard enough to cause the patient's chest to rise and fall.
• If the patient's chest fails to rise you need to adjust the position of the airway.
• The 16% of oxygen in your expired air is adequate to sustain life.
• Initially you need to give two full slow breaths.
• If the patient is found to have a pulse, in the next step continue breathing for the patient once every five seconds, checking for a pulse after every ten breaths.
• If the patient begins breathing on his own you can turn him/her into the recovery position.

Circulation
After giving the two breaths as above you now need to give external cardiac compression.
• Kneel next to the patient's chest
• Measure two finger breadths above the notch at the point where the ribs meet the lower end of the breast bone
• Place the heel of your left hand just above your two fingers in the centre of the breast bone
• Place heel of your right hand on your left hand
• Straighten your elbows
• Place your shoulders perpendicularly above the patient's breast bone
• Compress the breast bone 4 to 5cm to a rhythm

except when swallowing prey. They hang around on reefs and wrecks and pack a heavy sting in their beautiful spines.
Treatment: As for stonefish.

- **Rabbitfish** These have venomous spines in their fins, and should on no account be handled.
Treatment: Use the hot-water treatment.

- **Scorpionfish** Other scorpionfish are less camouflaged and less dangerous than the stonefish, but are more common and dangerous enough.
Treatment: As for stonefish.

- **Sea Snakes** Sea snakes have venom 10 times more powerful than a cobra's, but luckily they are rarely aggressive and their short fangs usually cannot pierce a wetsuit.
Treatment: Apply a broad ligature between the injury and the body and wash the wound. CPR may be necessary. Antivenins are available but need skilled medical supervision.

- **Sea Urchins** The spines of sea urchins can be poisonous. Even if not, they can puncture the skin – even through gloves – and break off, leaving painful wounds that often go septic.
Treatment: For bad cases give the hot-water treatment; this also softens the spines, helping the body reject them. Soothing creams or a magnesium-sulphate compress will help reduce the pain. Septic wounds require antibiotics.

- **Stinging Hydroids** Stinging hydroids often go unnoticed on wrecks, old anchor ropes and chains until you put your hand on them, when their nematocysts are fired into your skin. The wounds are not serious but are very painful, and large blisters can be raised on sensitive skin.
Treatment: Bathe the affected part in methylated spirit or vinegar (acetic acid). Local anaesthetic may be required to ease the pain, though antihistamine cream is usually enough.

- **Stinging Plankton** You cannot see stinging plankton, and so cannot take evasive measures. If there are reports of any in the area keep as much of your body covered as possible.
Treatment: As for stinging hydroids.

- **Sting Rays** Sting rays vary from a few centimtres to several metres across. The sting consists of one or more spines on top of the tail; though these point backwards they can sting in any direction. The rays thrash out and sting when trodden on or caught. Wounds may be large and severely lacerated.
Treatment: Clean the wound and remove any spines. Give the hot-water treatment and local anaesthetic if available; follow up with antibiotics and anti-tetanus.

- **Stonefish** Stonefish are the most feared, best camouflaged and most dangerous of the scorpionfish family. The venom is contained in the spines of the dorsal fin, which is raised when the fish is agitated.
Treatment: There is usually intense pain and swelling. Clean the wound, give the hot-water treatment and follow up with antibiotic and anti-tetanus.

- **Others** Venoms occur also in soft corals, the anemones associated with Clownfish and the nudibranchs that feed on stinging hydroids; if you have sensitive skin, do not touch any of them. Electric (torpedo) rays can give a severe electric shock (200–2000 volts); the main problem here is that the victim may be knocked unconscious in the water and drown.

Cuts

Underwater cuts and scrapes – especially from coral, barnacles or sharp metal – will usually, if not cleaned out and treated quickly, go septic; absorption of the resulting poisons into the body can cause bigger problems. After every dive, clean and disinfect any wounds, no matter how small. Larger wounds will often refuse to heal unless you stay out of seawater for a couple of days. Surgeonfish have sharp fins on each side of the caudal peduncle; they use these against other fish, lashing out with a sweep of the tail, and occasionally may likewise when defending territory against a trespassing diver. These 'scalpels' are often covered in toxic mucus, so wounds should be cleaned and treated with antibiotic cream. As a preventative measure against cuts in general, the golden rule is do not touch! Learn good buoyancy control so that you can avoid touching anything unnecessarily - remember, anyway, that every area of the coral you touch will be killed.

Fish-feeding

You should definitely not feed fish: you can harm them and their ecosystem. Not only that, it is dangerous to you, too. Sharks' feeding frenzies are uncontrollable, and sharks and groupers often bite light-coloured fins. Triggerfish can come at you very fast, and groupers and moray eels have nasty teeth. Napoleon Wrasse have strong mouth suction and can bite. Even little Sergeant Majors can give your fingers or hair a nasty nip.

Bryson, Dr P.J.: *Underwater Diving Accident Manual* (3rd edn 1993), Diving Diseases Research Centre, Plymouth, UK

Chou Loke Ming, and Porfirio, M. Alino: *An Underwater Guide to the South China Sea* (1992), Times Editions, Singapore

Dawood, Dr Richard: *Travellers' Health – How to Stay Healthy Abroad* (3rd edn 1992), Oxford University Press, Oxford, UK

Debelius, Helmut: *Southeast Asia Tropical Fish Guide* (1994), Ikan, Frankfurt, Germany

Eichler, Dieter and Lieske, Ewald (1994) *Korrallenfische Indischer Ozean*, Tauchen, Jahr Verlag Hamburg, Germany

Eliot, Joshua, Bickersteth, Jane, Miller, Jonathan, and Matthews, Georgina (eds): *Indonesia, Malaysia & Singapore Handbook* (1993 edn), Trade & Travel Publications, Bath, UK

George, J., and George, J. David: *Marine Life – An Illustrated Encyclopedia of Invertebrates in the Sea* (1979), Harrap, London, UK

Ho Soon Lin: *Coral Reefs of Malaysia* (1992), Tropical Press, Kuala Lumpur, Malaysia

Kuiter, Rudie H.: *Tropical Reef Fishes of the Western Pacific – Indonesia and Adjacent Waters* (1992), Gramedia, Jakarta

Lieske, Ewald and Myers, Robert (1994) *Collins Pocket Guide to Coral Reef Fishes of the Indo-Pacific and Caribbean*, Harper Collins, London

Myers, Robert F.: *Micronesian Reef Fishes* (2nd edn 1991), Coral Graphics, Barrigada, Guam

Oon, Helen: *Globetrotter Travel Guide Malaysia* (2000), New Holland, London

Sim Yong Wah, Captain: *Malaysia's Undersea Heritage* (1993), Discovery Editions, Kuala Lumpur

Stafford-Deitsch, Jeremy: *Reef – A Safari through the Coral World* (1991), Headline, London, UK

Stafford-Deitsch, Jeremy: *Shark – A Photographer's Story* (1987), Headline, London, UK

Veron, John Edward Norwood: *Corals of Australia and the Indo-Pacific* (1993), University of Hawaii Press, Hawaii

Wells, Sue, and Hanna, Nick: *The Greenpeace Book of Coral Reefs* (1992), Blandford, London, UK

Wells, Sue, et al.: *Coral Reefs of the World* (3 vols, 1988), United Nations Environmental Program/International Union for Conservation of Nature and Natural Resources, Gland, Switzerland

Wheeler, Tony, Finlay, Hugh, Turner, Peter, and Crowther, Geoff: *Malaysia, Singapore & Brunei – A Travel Survival Kit* (4th edn 1991), Lonely Planet Publications, Hawthorn, Victoria, Australia

White, Alan: *Philippine Coral Reefs – A Natural History Guide* (1987), New Day Publishers, Quezon City, Philippines

Wong, Michael Patrick: *Malaysia Beneath the Waves* (1997), Odyssey Publishing, Singapore

Wong, Michael Patrick: *Sipadan - Borneo's Underwater Paradise* (1991), Odyssey Publishing, Singapore

Wood, Elizabeth M.: *Corals of the World* (1983), T.F.H. Publications, Neptune, NJ, USA

WWF Malaysia: *The National Parks and Other Wild Places of Malaysia* (1998), New Holland, London

Index

Pulau Rawa 55, 83
Pulau Redang 58–63
Pulau Renggis 76
Pulau Sakijang Bendera 153
Pulau Salu 152
Pulau Sapi 98, 100
Pulau Satang Besar 87
Pulau Segantang 41
Pulau Selingan 120–21, 123
Pulau Serenggeh 53
Pulau Sipadan 95, 126–141
Pulau Sipidan Marine
   Reserve 126–33, 141
Pulau Suber Laut 153
Pulau Sudong 153
Pulau Sulug 98, 100
Pulau Susu Dara Besar 54
Pulau Susu Dara Kecil 55
Pulau Tenggol 66–71
Pulau Tiga Park 106–109
Pulau Tulai 74

Ray, Blue-spotted Ribbontail 96
Rabbitfish 173
Raffles Lighthouse 153
Recompression chambers 33
Regional directories 7
Regions 6
Rescue-location tube 33
Ron Reef 100

Sabah 10, 24
   East/Southeast coast 119–41
   Northwest coast 95–115
St John's Island 153
Sandakan 119
Sandy Ridge 145–6
Sangalaki 24, 143–9
Sapi Island 95, 101
Sapi Reef 100
Sarawak 10, 25, 87
Scorpionfish 173
Sea sickness 171
Sea Snakes 173
Sea Slug 143
Sea Squirt 143
Sea Stars 37, 101
Sea Urchins 101, 173
Seahorse 164
Sembilan Islands 39
Semporna Marine Park 124
Shallow-water cameras 165
Sharks 171–2
   Grey Reef 26, 172
   Hammerhead 26, 92
   Silvertip 26
   Leopard 26
   Whale 26
   Whitetip Reef Shark 26
Shipwreck, Pulau

Perhentian Kecil 53
Shock 171
Shrimps, Pistol 104
   Snapping 104
Singapore 151–5
   accommodation 21
   arriving in 20
   conservation in 161
   dangerous currents 151
   diving round 26
   electricity 21
   entry formalities 20
   geography 12
   getting around 21
   languages 13
   limited visibility 151
   money 20
   people 12–13
   visas 20
Sipadan 24
Sisters Island 153
Snapper 164
   Checkered 164
Snorkel, learning to 34–5
Snorkels 29–30
Soft Tree Corals 151
Soldierfish 164
   Blotch Eye 164
South China Sea 89
South Edgell Patch 99
South Point (Sipadan) 132
Sponge, Barrel 109
Spratlys, The 24, 89–93
Squirrelfish 164
   Redcoat 156
Staghorn Crest 132
Starfish, Crown-of-
   Thorns 64, 172
Sting Ray Patch 148
Sting Rays 173
Stinging Hydroids 173
Stinging Plankton 173
Stonefish 173
Sub-regions 6
Submersible cameras 165
Sulug Reef 100
Sunburn 171
Surprise Rock island 97
Swimmer's ear 171
Symbiosis 104–5
Symbols 7

Table Corals 65
Tanjung Batu Tokong 60
Tanjung Besi 50
Tanjung Butung 54
Tanjung Gua Kawah 60
Tanjung Panglima Abu 53
Tanjung Tukas 52
Teluk Air Tawar 70

Teluk Dalam (Perhentian) 52
Teluk Dalam (Redang) 60
Teluk Kerma 55
Teluk Pauh 50
Terembu Layang-Layang 92
Terengganu Marine
   Park 48–63, 66–71
Terengganu turtles 49
Terumbu Tiga 52
Tiga Ruang 50
Tiger Rocks 76
Tokong Bahara 76
Tokong Bopeng 55
Tokong Burong 68
Tokong Burung Kecil 55
Tokong Laut 54
Tokong Talang To Pulau 68
Transparent Cleaner Shrimp . . .104
Trevally 163
Triggerfish 164, 172
   Clown 67
   Orange Striped 164
Tropical diseases 171
Tubastrea Cup Coral 47
Tumbu Kili 62–3
Tunku Abdul Rahman Marine
   Park 96–103
Turkeyfish (Lionfish) 173
Turtle, Green . . .25, 80–81, 89, 121
   Hawksbill 80–81, 119
   Leatherback 59, 71, 80
   Pacific Olive Ridley 81
Turtle Bay 60
Turtle Cavern 130
Turtle Island 153
Turtle Islands Park 120–3
Turtle Patch (Sipadan) 131
Turtle Patch
   (Sangalaki) 146
Turtle Town 146
Turtles 60, 80–81, 127

Underwater photography . . .165–7

Vaccination, certificate of 15
Venomous sea creatures 172
Video 167
Violin Island 153

West Malaysia 10, 37–89
West Ridge 128
Whitetip Avenue and Mid
   Reef 131
Wrasse 164
   Cleaner 104
   Giant Humphead 164
Wreck diving 111, 114